From
Kickapoo to Kathmandu
(and everywhere in between)

Dedication

I dedicate this book to the loving memory of my father and mother, Roderick E. Olson and Patricia C. Olson. My Dad passed away to heaven on June 14th, 2021 as I was finishing this book. As a family we miss him and Mom very much.

I am grateful to my husband, family and friends who have supported and helped me in writing this book. Thank you, editors who have made this book readable!

From Kickapoo to Kathmandu
(and everywhere in between)

ADVENTURES OF GRACE ON THE SILK ROAD

PAMELA RANNIE LOVETT

Bridge Builders, LLC

From Kickapoo to Kathmandu
by Pamela Rannie Lovett

Copyright © 2021, Pamela Rannie Lovett

ISBN: 978-1-7379453-0-7

First Edition 2021

Published by
Pamela Rannie Lovett
Bridge Builders International, LLC
PO Box 581
Wales, WI 53183
USA

Bridge Builders, LLC
www.cqlovett.com

Cover design: Terry Dugan
Cover photos: from Unsplash.com
Background- Jeremy Zero
Shepherd - Patrick Schneider
Child- Aaron Santelices
Camel - Jeremy Zero
Woman- Simon Sun
Building - Shairyar Khan

Printed and bound in India by
Good Shepherd Media, Secunderabad 500 067, Telangana, India
e-mail: printing@ombooks.org

Contents

Acknowledgements

There are many people that I would like to thank in connection with making this book possible to go to the printing press. I especially, want to thank my husband David Lovett who has been very supportive and patient with me as I have been writing this book in the past few years, especially during the months of Covid-19 pandemic.

I want to thank my friends and family members who encouraged me to keep on with this project. Thank you to Lynne Green for reading this book in its rough draft form.

Thank you to Sally DiFrances for helping with the beginning stages of editing pages.

Thank you to KC Joseph for his coaching efforts to print this book from Good Shepherd Media.

Thank you to Deborah Meroff for the final versions of editing.

Last but not least, I want to thank God for His faithfulness He has shown to us. He has been my Rock and Salvation. Thank you to all friends and family.

Foreword

"I've never been to the Kickapoo but I have visited Kathmandu. Most people I know have been to neither but Pam Lovett was born in the former and she and her husband Dave have lived and worked for years in the latter and beyond. If a country's name ends in "Stan" meaning "land of" - like Tajikistan and Afghanistan - there's a good chance the Lovett's have lived there and left their mark. They have not spent the last 38 years climbing the Himalayas or looking for Noah's ark but rather looking for ways to bring the message of Christ as the source of blessing to people in need of physical, emotional, social and spiritual renewal and salvation. Their's is a story of hard work, dogged commitment, patience and undying faith and will bless anyone who, attracted by the book's title wants to know where the Kickapoo is, and discovers far more than they planned for."

Be blessed.

Stuart Briscoe,
Author, Broadcaster

Introduction

From Kickapoo to Kathmandu (and everywhere in between)

Adventures of grace on the Silk Road

As the years have gone by since my birth in 1959 until 2006, a lot has happened in my life. I grew up in a farming horseback riding community in Wisconsin. I rode horses as much as I could in the pasture lands and rugged hilly terrain of the Kickapoo Valley until I went to college. Attending church was part of our farming culture, so we went to a Lutheran church. I became a Christian at a Lutheran youth rally in 1977. When high school finished, I worked for a year before college at Bethany Global University in Minneapolis, Minnesota. I went to study the Bible

11

but then realized that training for going into missions was what I wanted to do.

While I was there, I met this suburban young man from New Jersey named David Lovett. We married after college in 1982 and decided to live and work overseas, starting in India. We also lived in Bangladesh and then Pakistan. We pioneered a humanitarian development work in the landlocked rugged mountainous region of Tajikistan just north of Afghanistan.

Over the years, as we have lived in these different countries, we have seen God be so faithful to us. We prayed that God would help us to remain faithful to serve Him and help others come to know Christ. We lived in challenging conditions so very different from how we grew up in the USA.

In India, we experienced the violent riots in New Delhi when Indira Gandhi was killed by her personal bodyguards. Our apartment was just behind the All Indian Medical Institute, where her body was taken to revive. We traveled to Pakistan for a short time to hike up into the mountainous regions to spread the gospel to people who had never heard about Jesus. After about three months, we went back to India, but we couldn't get a visa to stay in the country long-term.

In 1986, we went to Bangladesh to work at the mission training center. In 1987, our daughter was born at a mission hospital near where today the Rohingya refugees are encamped. In 1988, we moved to Pakistan, worked with Afghan refugees, and started to learn the Dari language. We left that region to go back to the States for the birth of our second child because I had become very sick with this pregnancy.

In 1993, we began to pioneer work in Tajikistan, a very mountainous region that suffered a war that finally finished in 1998. We saw God provide for us in remarkable ways. We had the privilege to see people come to know Christ; we enjoyed many friends with many people in that country. The hospitality of these mountain people was truly amazing. They would give anything off their backs to help someone. After the war, we enjoyed several years of peace before moving back to the states in 2006.

We definitely saw God's faithfulness to us all those years of serving him in very difficult areas of the world. He is our gracious Shepherd wherever He has led us to serve others.

God is at work everywhere and helps His people.

God met me, opened my eyes, and gave me a new heart to serve Him in the rugged hills of the Kickapoo Valley, Wisconsin. In the same way, I believe that He is all about helping "the least reached peoples" to come to Christ in remote areas like the far off valleys in the rugged mountainous regions in the world.

CHAPTER 1

Out of the Depths

On both sides of our family I am largely descended from the indigenous people of Norway. For centuries these folk survived by fishing, fur trapping, sheep, cattle or reindeer herding and living simply off the land.

In the late 1800's my great grandparents emigrated to America from the Ardal region of Norway, looking for new opportunities. Jacob Hoffland, the son of another Jacob, sailed across the Atlantic Ocean and through the St. Lawrence Seaway to Milwaukee, Wisconsin. From there his family continued by train to Madison, then took an ox cart to the Norwegian settlement in Soldiers Grove.

My second great grandfather, Lewis Knutson (who had changed his name from Thorson), left Stavangar, Norway, as a teenager. After arriving in America through Ellis Island he also made his way overland to Southwestern Wisconsin and Soldiers Grove.

This community had been pioneered in 1856 by Joseph Brightman, who built a sawmill to process logs rafted down the nearby Kickapoo River. The village that sprang up near the sawmill was first called Pine Grove because of the abundant growth of Eastern White Pine trees in the area. That name was changed to Soldiers Grove in 1867, to commemorate troops that camped there during a conflict with native Indians.

Norwegian immigrants worked hard to carve a new life for themselves in the river valley and the rough, hilly terrain of the Ocooch Mountains. Unfortunately, like their forefathers, many individuals were vulnerable to alcohol addiction.

I was born out-of-wedlock when my mother, the youngest of eight children, was only seventeen years old. My grandmother, who was a daughter of a farmer involved in the Norwegian Lutheran church started up in the region, was then married to a productive farmer. Unfortunately he periodically went on alcohol binges, and she refused to allow my mother to marry a young man with the same bad habit.

I later learned from my adoptive father that Mom's boyfriend was mean to her when she fell pregnant with me. My Dad, who was then only a friend at the time, protected her once when he was roughing her up. Grandma knew the heartaches of this lifestyle and was determined to protect her daughter. Mom went on to finish high school while my grandparents took care of me during school hours. Later I learned from one of her friends that many of my mother's fellow students respected her very much for continuing her education, even while pregnant.

My mother is my hero, because she endured the cattiness and gossip so typical of small towns where nearly everyone is related.

In time she married Roderick Earl Olson, a good man who accepted me as his own, although I was too young to know this at the time.

I was the eldest child and grew up with two half-sisters, Gail and Kally. We three Olson girls were well known for riding our horses all over the valley. Our parents ran a farm of 160 acres, growing corn, oats, hay and tobacco and raising cattle and horses. They also operated a small Mobil gas and repair station.

Spending my childhood in the Kickapoo River Valley, where my great grandparents and other relatives had settled, I learned the value of hard work. I helped my parents with daily ranch chores, the housework and their small business. My Dad taught me how to train horses from around the age of six, so I often handled them when I wasn't in the fields or doing other farm work. Often I practiced the horses on pole bending, barrel racing, figure eight barrels and Texas flag race for horse competitions. There was always plenty of fun to be had with my sisters, cousins, neighbors and friends. Besides riding we enjoyed hotdog roasts over an open fire, canoeing, sledding, ice skating, hunting, fishing, snowmobiling, dancing or watching sports events.

Back when I was in the third grade, I was walking home from school one day when a classmate told me I was adopted. Shocked to the core, I rushed into the house to ask my mom if this was true. She said it was. I didn't know how to handle this revelation.—Didn't know who I was anymore. I felt angry. Betrayed. I could not let go of my feelings and couldn't talk to anyone about them.

Going into my teen years I was still troubled, though I managed to maintain good grades, compete on the basketball and track teams and win ribbons at horse-riding events. Whenever I had a chance I took long trail rides with my friends or cousins, across hills and valleys and on gravel roads in the backwoods.

Sometimes Dad and Mom took us boating and waterskiing on the Mississippi River. We invited others to go with us, and Mom cooked picnics on the beach. A highlight of the summer was spending time on an island of the Mississippi, playing games in the water. But a longing for love and acceptance from others led me to make unhealthy choices. I got involved in bad relationships and began partying, using drugs and getting drunk. I even dabbled with the occult. In the end, everything I tried left me feeling empty.

One night when I was seventeen I was joyriding around town with friends when the police stopped our car. A search turned up marijuana in the trunk. I had no idea it was there. Although the substance was illegal then, charges were eventually dropped. The incident shook me.

Another time, before I had decided to stop drinking so much because of next-day hangovers, I remember walking home with a boyfriend down the main street of Soldiers Grove. The village boasted several bars and was known as the go-to place to drink. That night I was so drunk I could hardly stand up. As we staggered along the street and then up and over the hill towards my parents' house, just over a mile away, I fell down. My face struck the curb, hitting my upper cheek bone just below my eye so hard that it scraped my skin.

My boyfriend made sure that I finally got home, where I immediately started to vomit in the bathroom off the kitchen. The dry heaves wrenched my insides until I gladly fell into bed. I don't know how long I slept, but the next day I knew I couldn't keep drinking so much. It was way too hard on my body.

I believed in God. I even went to church because it was expected in our little community, but I had never known Him in a personal way. Now for some reason I felt drawn to read the Bible, compelled by a hunger I didn't understand.

My friend who was originally from Illinois had a Christian grandmother, and this Mrs. Werthwien had told him that a good place to start reading the Bible was in the book of Romans. So that's where I started.

One afternoon this friend and I were out partying and driving around the hills just east of Soldiers Grove. We were high on some drug when I was suddenly startled to hear a voice, telling me that I was going to change and go to live in a clean and wholesome society.

I asked my companion if he had heard the same voice, and he said yes. I am sure his grandma had been praying for him and possibly for me, too, at that moment.

Little did I know that my own aunt and uncle in Texas were also intently praying for me! Later I learned that my mom had committed me to the Lord as she saw the trouble I was in as a teen. She realized she couldn't change me by her own efforts, and asked God to take control of my life.

Thankfully, He answered those prayers. On a bitter cold, snowy day in January 1977 our Lutheran church's youth group travelled to a youth rally in Minneapolis. My whole family went along. I remember that night as if it was yesterday. At the end of the message the speaker asked people in the audience to come forward for prayer, and I sensed the strong, electrifying power of the Holy Spirit compelling me to the front of that auditorium.

Counselors stood waiting to pray with us. As I walked up to one of them, I asked if smoking pot was wrong. He probably wasn't expecting such a question, but gladly prayed with me and led me to the waiting arms of Jesus Christ. As I surrendered my life and made Him my Lord and Savior, I experienced overwhelming joy and peace in my life for the first time. I had finally found the love I was looking for: the eternal, all powerful, accepting love of Jesus. I knew my life would never be the same.

I am so grateful that Jesus accepts all people, even from the roughest backgrounds. God is a redeeming God and can redeem any mess we make of our lives. He changed my heart that night. I now had hope, peace and a true purpose to live.

Jesus tells people so clearly, "I am the Way, the Truth and the Life, and no man can come to the father except through me." Without Him, life does not make sense. Wild partying and living just to have a good time eventually becomes boring and unfulfilling. On the other hand, living with the goal of "loving the Lord your God with all your heart, mind, and strength and loving your neighbor as yourself" brings joy unspeakable. It is what we are born for.

CHAPTER 2

Make Me Thy Fuel

My behavior after I gave my life to Christ was so dramatically changed that my teachers suspected I was high on drugs. I continued to attend my family's church but I also visited other churches in a different town to check them out. My pastor's wife helped me enroll in a Bible correspondence study because they had to move away to another parish. Then for a while our church had substitute pastors come in to conduct services. Nobody had to tell me to share my faith. It was good news for me to spread around to the others, because Jesus changed me so much for the better. As I competed in my school's track and field events for the fourth year I ran for the Lord and to honor my parents. My coaches voted me the most valued—and most improved—player.

Following high school I attended a six-week "Agape Force" training camp that was meant to disciple young believers. Along with other young people I committed total control of my life to

Jesus. My first move after that was to make restitution to all the people I had wronged in the past.

That winter I used all the money I had earned working on the farm to attend a course run by Youth With A Mission (YWAM), in Hawaii. There I was stunned at the possibilities open to me to serve God in countries around the world.

As a child I had gotten to visit Canada and Mexico with my parents. This was an eye-opening experience for a Wisconsin farm girl. I was fascinated by the variations in language, living conditions, food, clothing and transportation. Other than that I had little exposure to cultures outside my own, narrow world, except for what I learned from my Aunt Judy and Uncle Lawrence. They had been missionaries to Colombia and I always respected the fact that they were godly people who never swore or drank.

Now I was ready to offer my own life for service wherever God might choose. Enrolling at Bethany College of Missions in Minneapolis, known today as Bethany Global University, seemed the next logical step. The school described itself as a missions college dedicated to training missionaries to take the church where it is not. My two uncles, Lawrence Knutson and Maurice Thoftne encouraged me to attend this college to get an education in the areas of communications and Bible theology. This proved to be wise advice. At Bethany I was grounded in the Word of God and greatly improved my English grammar, writing and public speaking skills.

I thoroughly enjoyed getting to know other students at Bethany, who hailed from all parts of the United States as well as the world. My freshman roommate from the East Coast definitely grew up differently from me, and I was resolved to help her change for the better, in my opinion. She was the messy one in our room and I was the neat one. Part of my education that year was to learn to accept my friend as she was, and not try to change her.

I remember that whenever we had room inspection to check for cleanliness and tidiness, we were both disciplined and put on dishwashing duty. I felt this wasn't fair and complained that my part of the room was perfectly orderly. Why should I be disciplined when the problem was hers? In the end the staff stopped giving us dishwashing duty for our somewhat messy quarters. I will say that when my roommate was disciplined for her mess, she began to pick up her stuff more often.

When it came to study times, I chose to use the campus library. I felt cooped up in our small dormitory room, being so used to wide open spaces and the freedom of roaming around on the farm, on horseback.

In fact, during my studies at Bethany I suffered a lot from homesickness. One time I talked about this with my mom on the in the chapel foyer telephone. I wanted so badly to leave school and go home to Soldiers Grove, but Jesus wouldn't let me go. I could hear Him saying in my heart, "Stay here with me." I did as He said and looking back, I am so glad that I stuck it out at Bethany Fellowship, even though I didn't have the emotional backing of my family. Now they do seem glad that I got a college education. Jesus has so patiently continued to teach me His ways! They are certainly better than any ways I or the world could devise.

While I was at Bethany my grandfather, Tillman Knutson, on my mom's side of the family passed away, and my younger sister Gail got married. She was the first of us to get married so I was thankful to be able to go home for her wedding. My grandmother, Beatrice Rannie Knutson died just before this, my third year of college when I was in Miami and Puerto Rico for my internship.

The mission projects Bethany supported around the world challenged my heart. They had a Bible school and a book publishing work in Brazil, bookstores in Mexico, Puerto Rico and Miami, Florida and other outreaches in various countries. In order to improve their students' intercultural skills they were assigned a practical year of ministry outside their comfort zones.

For my first six months I worked at the Miami bookstore. Living in the staff house I learned the importance of developing and maintaining healthy friendships with team members, as well as with customers who came into the store. I served in the sales department and one customer told me that whenever he came into the store not really planning to buy anything, he always walked out with a purchase that I had persuaded him would be good to have.

After Wisconsin, Florida struck me as very flat. I lived there in the fall and did see that the state had some seasonal changes, however. I also observed that many residents came from the Caribbean or South America and spoke Spanish.

After a while, working, eating, cleaning, going to church and hanging out with my team members was a bit too much togetherness. We didn't always see eye to eye. But one woman in the team, Fran Flanagan, had formerly been a Catholic nun and I loved talking with her about God. She is the one who taught me how to play the guitar and also encouraged me to keep persevering in learning. I loved her upbeat positive attitude towards life. Fran always reminded me, "there is joy in anticipation!"

To my surprise, halfway through my internship I was transferred to a second assignment in Puerto Rico. I thought going to the Caribbean was a great opportunity and did enjoy this change of scenery as well as being with a new team.

My main job at my new mission station was washing dishes and cleaning the facilities. Working on the cleaning team didn't bother me at all because I learned new ways of doing things in the tropics. I was also trained to help out with book tables at church services. There were dozens of churches all over the islands and I loved travelling around with the team, seeing more of the countryside and how people lived. Puerto Ricans were very laid-back culturally: friendly, talkative and hospitable. Some lived in poverty, in tin shacks; others had very nice homes.

The islands were tropical, with a wide variety of trees and vegetation growing like weeds did in fields back home. When I went hiking with some of my team members I saw another area that was very dry and volcanic.

Mosquitos were everywhere. The room that the team gave me did not have window screens, although I always left the windows open at night to keep cool since there was no air conditioning. After a while I came down with dengue fever, a mosquito-borne disease like malaria. The high fever, muscle and joint pain made me so weak that I could hardly sit up, walk or even sweep a floor with a light broom.

One of the missionaries cared for me during my illness and I don't remember ever taking so much aspirin and Tylenol in my life. People have died from severe forms of dengue fever, but even though it took me several weeks, God in His mercy allowed me to recover completely. I was so glad to finally feel my strength come back. But after this experience I hoped God would never call me back to work in the tropics!

While I was in Puerto Rico I tried to learn Spanish, though I wasn't very successful. I did enjoy helping children with their English skills, however. Some of the boys and girls who came onto the compound liked to talk with me while I swam in the mission's pool. They called me Palm instead Pam and it tickled me to hear their pronunciation when it was such a simple name. I got used to their accent and enjoyed the children's company.

While I was on my internship, a relationship that I had developed with a young man back at Bethany came to an end. We both agreed over a long distant telephone call that it wasn't going to work out, as he didn't share my vision to make a positive difference among the poor in countries outside the USA. I was glad that we were able to say goodbye to each other with friendly feelings instead of resentment. Bitterness would surely have eaten away at our hearts otherwise, and life is too short to hold onto grudges through unforgiveness.

After my intern practicum year with the mission training program was finished, I went back to campus to go through a debriefing and finish up my classes. This allowed me to ask questions about my field experiences in Florida and a Latino area of the world, across the waters. I can say that I really did enjoy this exposure to other cultures. Many positive things can be said about "short term" missions, and I wouldn't have traded such valuable training for anything. God was stretching me mentally and physically for what lay ahead.

During our year at Bethany we students could be part of a work program that helped to pay for our tuition. I had been part of many departments like the campus kitchen crew and cleaning crew, the public laundry room, professional carpet cleaning and a camping trailer factory. I had also been a book shipper in the publishing department, called Bethany House. I learned so much from all these experiences. Before the crews started their work we all gathered in our departments for a short devotional and prayer. What a beautiful time of learning it was. Dave, who I mention below, also had a variety of jobs during his four years of college. Besides helping in the Bethany House printshop he was a night guard for the campus and work departments and learned professional carpet cleaning and waxing of floors.

Reconnecting with classmates as they came from their own intern assignments that year was a joy. We all had lots of stories to share with each other. A few students joined our class from a two-year practicum on the field. Dave Lovett and Jim Rasmussen had been serving in the South Asian subcontinent with Operation Mobilization (OM). They had no end of riveting stories about their travels in India and Pakistan. At student-led prayer meetings they gave us exciting insights about what God was doing overseas, before we prayed for each situation. What a challenge to our hearts to hear news that would never make CNN, FOX or local networks. I confess that in those days I hardly listened to the news anyway, too busy studying, working and building friendships.

I was enriched by my opportunity to study at Bethany Fellowship. The school laid a strong foundation for my faith in Jesus. I learned how to study the Bible in depth. I also learned that prayer was the backbone to ministry, the "war room" where most of the action takes place. On campus I regularly attended intercessory prayer times for missionaries and critical situations in various countries. We saw evidence of those prayers releasing God's hands to push back evil forces.

During my last year of campus life God increased my interest in going to India. My roommate, Salma Carunia, was from the southern part of that country, growing up in an orphanage founded by Amy Carmichael in Dohnavur. She was a teacher in that mission as well. I had read about Amy Carmichael's life and learned more from some Sunday School materials when I was teaching children. Amy's 56 years of serving in India without a furlough, caring for children rescued from temple prostitution, impacted me in such a profound way. Her life story has always encouraged me to keep pressing on in helping the poor and oppressed. So sharing our last year together was good training for me. The cross cultural issues I learned by living with an Indian helped to prepare me for moving to a country so different from America.

That same year I started getting to know Dave Lovett, who was originally from New Jersey before coming to Bethany. I was totally fascinated by his mission adventures on Indian outreach teams. In many cases the villages where they preached the gospel had never before heard of Jesus Christ. In fact, it was the first time many of the villagers had ever seen a white person in their midst!

As our senior year at Bethany College of Missions progressed I became interested in Dave himself, but didn't think that anything would ever come of it. I continued faithfully attending classes, prayer meetings and work assignments. After doing homework I hung out with friends, joining outreaches to the Minneapolis community in order to extend Jesus' love.

I remember wishing I could share my desire to go to India with my home church, but I wasn't so sure that they would get behind me. Most people in a small-town country church didn't have a big vision for missions.

I really didn't know how I was going to get financial and prayer support to go with Operation Mobilisation for a year or two. Before going to college I had attended an educational seminar with Youth With a Mission at one of their training schools in Hawaii, paying for that trip with my own earnings from a tobacco harvest. I had received the check after my sister and I sold the crop to a tobacco company, with Dad's help. So having come up with funds before without the church's help, it didn't seem likely they would give me support for the longer-term mission I wanted to do.

Throughout the spring of 1982, Dave and I continued to get to know each other more deeply. We had been raised very differently; Dave was a city boy from outside New York City and

I had grown up in the country. I was the oldest of an all-girl family while he was the second child in a family with two brothers and two sisters. Like me, Dave had been saved by Jesus from a lifestyle of substance abuse. But I knew that if our relationship was to work we would both need to make adjustments in learning how to get along with each other.

Graduation arrived in May. Both of our parents had come to the graduation weekend ceremony—Bill and Anne Lovett from Berkeley Heights, New Jersey; and my parents, Roderick and Patricia C. Olson from Soldiers Grove, Wisconsin.

At this point, Dave wasn't sure if he wanted to marry me. He kept saying that we were just friends. So when he suggested that our parents meet up, I felt it was a bit odd. Maybe he was more serious than what he was letting on?

Anyway, both sets of parents met and enjoyed each other's company. George Hermann, Dave's elderly Christian mentor from New Jersey, also came to our graduation. I found out later that after sweet, silver gray-haired and twinkly-eyed George met me, he said to Dave, "What are you waiting for?" The rest is history, as you will see.

After our graduation from Bethany College of Missions that spring we both continued on with the summer work program, in a dating mode. I was pretty sure at this time that we should get married, but Dave still wasn't, so I let the situation rest and gave my desire to God.

Meanwhile I had not seen any support come in to go to India, and doubted I would ever get help from my home church. Dave and I continued to see each other, wanting to know each other better before he was supposed to leave for India with OM. He had raised all the necessary support.

In the middle of the summer of 1982, Dave decided to date me more seriously. We called my parents back on the farm in the

Soldiers Grove, Wisconsin, and Dave asked Dad and Mom if he could date me with serious intensions.

Dad responded jocularly, "Sure, we think you are a pretty doggone good guy!"

That was great news for me, because that meant they liked him a lot.

In July, Dave was still uncertain about marrying me before returning to India as a single man. He went to one of the pastors at the college to get some advice on his dilemma. The pastor was Alec Brooks, who had been our doctrines teacher during our years at Bethany.

Alec simply asked Dave, "Why don't you just get married and go to India together? Then you can grow together."

Dave thought that was a good idea. Later that month Dave proposed to me in a hayfield, and I said yes. Even though he warned me that we wouldn't have an easy life or mod cons like a washing machine, refrigerator, comfortable bed and nice clothes, it didn't bother me. I already knew how to live without modern conveniences.

Growing up, I had had to work hard in the hay and tobacco fields. I had trained horses, taken care of cattle and lived without air conditioning in our house when it was hot and humid outside. But although I had worked short-term in Puerto Rico with its own poverty problems, mosquito-ridden illnesses and high humidity, I had not yet experienced the depth of poverty and unrelenting climate I would experience in the subcontinent.

I was overjoyed to say yes to Dave's marriage proposal that day, in the unmown hayfield across the road from Bethany Fellowship's property. Since neither of us had a lot of money, we chose to go to a jeweler just down the road to choose our wedding rings. We bought them at a good price, befitting our budget as poor students.

I was accepted into OM in the fall of 1982 as we continued to make plans for our wedding on October 23. Although we dreamed of having at least seven children, I didn't want to get pregnant on my first year of marriage. We wanted to get to know each other better before the kids came along.

Our special day finally came around, and the wedding took place at Our Saviors Lutheran Church in Soldiers Grove. Dave's family members and friends travelled to Wisconsin from New Jersey for the occasion, and many of my friends and family members joined us. A bus load of other friends from Bethany College of Missions also drove the four to five-hour journey to be with us. We were so happy to be surrounded by so much love.

During the ceremony, Dave and I chose to sing a song written by missionary to India Amy Carmichael, called "Flame of God." Accompanied by a guitarist we sang it together in front of everyone, me in my wedding dress and Dave in his suit. I am still praying the words in these verses:

From prayer that asks that I may be
Sheltered from winds that beat on Thee,
From fearing when I should aspire,
From faltering when I should climb higher
From silken self, O Captain, free
Thy soldier who would follow Thee.

From subtle love of softening things,
From easy choices, weakenings,
(Not thus are spirits fortified,
Not this way went the Crucified)
From all that dims Thy Calvary
O Lamb of God, deliver me.

Give me the love that leads the way,
The faith that nothing can dismay

The hope no disappointments tire,
The passion that will burn like fire;
Let me not sink to be a clod;
Make me Thy fuel, Flame of God

After the ceremony we took a few weeks off to honeymoon in the northern part of Wisconsin and Minnesota. After spending several days in cabins we decided to drive back to visit my side of the family before travelling down to the Ozarks to go camping. Unfortunately, we didn't know it was deer hunting season. One morning we woke up, stepped out of the tent onto the first snow of the season and found men walking around in orange deer hunting clothes. We decided our camping trip was over. We headed back to the East Coast to be with Dave's side of the family in New Jersey before taking the next step overseas.

We actually ended up living with Dave's parents for about nine months, raising more support and preparing for our first assignment together in cross cultural work.

We knew that our heavenly Father was doing His own preparation work for all He had in mind for us to do. Little did we guess that He would take us to many countries besides India. This was just the beginning of our adventures with God!

CHAPTER 3

Far From the Green, Green Grass of Home

It was OM Director George Verwer who advised us to take a year getting used to married life, before heading to India. After living with Dave's parents for most of those months we arranged many meetings around the States to share about our intended ministry. The goal was not only to raise adequate financial support but to build a solid core of churches and individuals committed to praying for us on the field.

After a final visit to my family in Wisconsin we flew to Leuven, Belgium, in the fall of 1983. There we joined other Operation Mobilization staff and recruits who would be working both short and long term on various fields, at an orientation conference. Besides being blessed by excellent Bible teaching and taking part in intercessory prayer meetings, we benefited from information and training about the new cultures we would each be facing.

The food served at the old, brick and wood conference building majored on bread and soup. For this farm girl who grew up with hearty meals of meat, potatoes and veggies, this was a dietary downgrade. However, we survived, and it was all part of GMT—Good Missionary Training—as we liked to joke. The fellowship with believers from all over the world more than made up for the basic amenities.

Dave and I were pleased to meet with Ray Eicher, who was the acting OM India director at that time. Ray and Christa Eicher were veteran workers in the subcontinent, among the first pioneers. We discussed the role he wanted us to fill in Delhi, which was running a hospitality house. He explained that it was essential to have a couple overseeing a place to stay for all the workers who continually transitted in and out of India.

I think Ray was wondering how I would manage this challenge, since I had never been to India before and didn't really know what I was getting into. I remember telling him that when you are training a horse, you have to get on the animal's back to start the process. If you fall off, you simply need to climb back onto the horse and start again.

I think he realized then that I meant business about adapting to life in Delhi. I have learned that attitude is a big part of determining how well we persevere through life's challenges.

At the end of the conference we all devoted a day of prayer for the finances still needed to cover the expense of everyone's flight tickets, visas and other arrangements. Eventually our tickets were booked and off we went to the airport. About twelve of us were heading to Delhi, the capital of the predominantly Hindu nation of India. Some would then disperse to other destinations.

The flight was long and crowded, but I remember being encouraged that we were in the company of other OM volunteers. Once we arrived in the capital city of over 11 million souls, we faced daunting immigration controls. Slowly we shuffled forward in long lines, hot and exhausted and wondering when and if we would ever make it through.

Suddenly one of the gals from South Africa was pulled aside. She was informed she had to go into quarantine because of yellow fever problems in her home country. Since South Africa didn't have any such problems, she was shocked and devastated to be separated from the rest of us. Eventually she was released to rejoin us, but it was a scare for her and for me, too. We had never before been confronted by such arbitrary behavior from airport officials.

We all breathed a sigh of relief when we finally stepped out of the airport into a sunny, though foggy, early morning. We had been met by a young Englishman named Stephen Ball as we left the baggage control area. He assigned three of our number to take charge of everyone's luggage and accompany him in several motorized rickshaws: three-wheeled vehicles that are one of the primary modes of transport in India. The rest of us would have to take a bus to the district of Gautam Nagar, where the OM apartment was.

I traveled with two other women on the bus. While it was exciting to be in a new and very exotic place, getting to the apartment without Dave was an intimidating prospect. We really didn't know where we were going in that gigantic city, and we didn't even have cell phones in those days, in case we got lost. But we were so tired we really didn't even think about that possibility. All of the new sights and sounds around us were overwhelming. I remember the other gals and I were in a hilarious mood, unable to contain our laughter over the insane way we had been picked up to join our team.

I remember when we finally got off the bus and started walking down an overcrowded, filthy street toward the apartment. I kept telling myself that this couldn't be the way, but it was. Poverty like I had never seen before stared me in the face. Dirt and trash littered the pavements and people had urinated along the wall lining the street, leaving a horrendously pungent smell.

The hospitality apartment was on the second floor of an unimpressive-looking building. It was made up of four rooms but no hallways. The two front rooms had doors to a front porch which went around to the back two bedrooms; these had doors to a back porch open to the elements. The kitchen was on this back porch along with two shower rooms and two eastern-style, stand-up toilets. There was no refrigerator. Single men had been living in the place and had been using kerosene burners for cooking, as well as electric burners. Grimy, black soot covered the kitchen walls. Opening the window that swung towards the apartment's open back porch triggered a tsunami of cockroaches scurrying to get away. The apartment obviously hadn't been cleaned in a very long time..

We needed to use nets over our beds because of the swarms of mosquitos occupying the space. Only a block away hundreds of people lived in the dirty tents and makeshift brick shacks of a very poor slum. The main garbage heap for our neighborhood was in the same direction. This part of Dehli didn't have very many trees and the streets were clouded with dust from passing traffic. Because so many apartments were stacked so close to each other and the walls were so thin we could hear the loud conversations of our neighbors and hear the television or radio programs they were enjoying.

Dave and I had no choice but to roll up our sleeves. We scrubbed and tidied and rearranged the sparse furnishings as best we could, even eventually painting the windowless kitchen.

The extreme heat and humidity didn't help, and unfortunately it didn't take long for the black soot from the kerosene burners to darken the walls again. One of our first purchases was an ice cooler to store basics like milk, butter and leftovers.

It was all an important lesson in keeping our eyes on Jesus, the author and finisher of our faith. As we learned to trust Him in all circumstances, He gave us the strength and will to overcome.

The thing that most struck me during my first weeks in India was the throngs of people on the streets at all hours of the day and night. A constant cacophony filled the air with pedestrians shouting, car horns blaring and bike dingers going off. Wild dogs, pigs and cows also had the run of the streets. How I missed the quiet sounds of the countryside where I was from!

I discovered I needed to change my wardrobe from western clothes to a loose-fitting *shalwar kameez* (a long tunic over loose fitting slacks) and sarees. These outfits were cooler and did not make me stand out so much as a foreigner. I had to get used to shopping in the open air *bazaars* that sold vegetables, fruit, meat, spices and grains at individual stalls. This was a very noisy area. My neighbors, after we became friends, taught me how to shop and bargain at the bazaar. Many times Dave and I went together to buy what we needed.

I observed many ornate Hindu temples in different locations. They always had flowers and food stalls nearby for worshippers to buy and offer to idols as sacrifices. It gave me an eerie feeling to walk by them. India had so many thousands of gods! They were a religious people, yet so many were in distress both physically and spiritually.

Fortunately I really liked the curried foods that became a regular part of our diet. My favorite dish was an egg curry; kebabs--fish, water buffalo or beef--were also very tasty. Of course everything was heavily spiced but this didn't bother me.

Many guests came through our crackerjack box apartment, even though it was so small. OM team members often came to Delhi to get visas, airplane or train tickets for other countries they were travelling to. Sometimes they needed to get medical help at the hospitals. I remember a particular young man who came to stay at our place, very sick with some type of dysentry problem. Dave and I tried to get him help but he never wanted to drink enough liquids to recover from the dehydration he was suffering. We cooked many meals in order to build his strength and it was a scary time of not knowing whether he would survive. But, thankfully, the man finally recovered enough to get on a plane and return to his home country.

Dave and I hosted over 500 men and women who came through our little apartment for various reasons. We regularly met with another team in Delhi for prayer meetings. This group was reaching out to help the many Afghan refugees who emigrated to the city, and we enjoyed having fellowship with them. Sometimes we went together for picnics in the parks.

After we been in Delhi for a few weeks we made a trip to the northern city of Lucknow to visit some of the OM team and directors in that region. The mission had a training center there for young people who wanted to study the Bible. The students were then sent out on teams to minister to churches and get involved in sharing the good news of Jesus' love by literature distribution. We traveled to Lucknow in a van with some single foreign women and a single Indian fellow. The vehicle was old and suffered two flat tires during the trip, which was only supposed to take a day. Both incidents could have been fatal, but by God's grace we survived the blowouts as the van barreled down the road.

The journey gave us the opportunity of stopping in Agra at the Taj Mahal, to view one of the great wonders of the world. The

Taj was the burial place of Emperor Shah Jahan's beloved wife, who died in childbirth in the 1600's. The Persian architectural design was breathtaking. The Shah employed 20,000 craftsmen and according to a horrifying but unsubstantiated local legend the main architect was killed so the mausoleum couldn't be replicated anywhere else. As one hears of the evil and selfishness that dominates much of our world, God's all-encompassing love and His offer of new life through Jesus is surely a breath of fresh air.

After we had left the Taj Mahal we resumed our trip with the goal of arriving in Lucknow that night. But then the van blew its second tire. Although we were able to get it fixed it was too dark to keep going on the narrow, treacherous roads. We decided to stop at a local tea shop where others had parked for the night. Dave and the Indian brother slept outside the van on woven rope beds, and the girls and I stayed inside the van. Needless to say the only toilet facilities available—mud and cement outhouses—left much to be desired. But early the next morning the little tea shop served us a welcome breakfast and hot *chai*—a sweet, milky tea usually spiced with cardamom--before we went on our way

The first day on the road—October 23--had happened to coincide with Dave's and my first wedding anniversary, by Indian subcontinent time. Despite the Biblical saying that where two or three are gathered Jesus is in their midst, Jesus' company is the only one really welcome on such an occasion!

However, our small traveling team made it safely to Lucknow on the second day of the journey, and that night we got to celebrate our first anniversary by US time. We stayed in an OM guest room, and after a meal with the team Dave and I enjoyed a bit of private, alone-time. It didn't matter so much that our grey-walled room with dim fluorescent lights wasn't the Hilton!

God definitely had His protective hand on us during that trip, and on the countless other journeys we took in the subcontinent. I have learned to pray, "O God, please help me to see what You are doing in me, around me and through me" at such times. And—oh, yes—"make me thankful!"

At the Lucknow OM base we were introduced to veteran workers Mike and Heather Wheate from the UK. They were involved in mentoring many of the young people at the training center. I asked Heather all kinds of questions about how to operate a hospitality house and keep it clean while surrounded by so much dirt and dust.

When we got back to our OM apartment in Delhi I continued to glean advice on India life from fellow team members, Christian Indian neighbors who lived above us--Frank and Helen Suttle, who were also in Christian ministry--and from another Christian Indian family, Enoch and Carunia Anthony with their two girls. I really enjoyed getting to know these families. Carunia had grown up in the orphanage that Amy Carmichael had started in South India. I learned so much from them about prayer and making myself available to others. Whenever I visited them unannounced they always made time for me. I was so impressed by the tireless hospitality they showed to so many people.

Carunia reminded me that when I got a house helper I should train them so they could get a good job with someone else later on. She knew that I probably wouldn't stay in India forever and she was right, of course. But I didn't know that then.

When we were living in the Gautam Nagar district, Indira Gandhi was India's prime minister. In June 1984 Gandhi ordered military intervention against extremist Sikhs, resulting in serious damage to the Sikhs' sacred Golden Temple in Amritsar, Punjab. Many pilgrims were killed. The action was widely criticized and fomented a conspiracy to take Gandhi's life. Although her Sikh body regards were removed out of security concerns, the prime minister herself had them reinstated, believing the men to be loyal. This was a fatal mistake, for on October 31 her two Sikh bodyguards emptied their guns into Gandhi as she walked to her office from an adjoining bungalow.

We happened to be travelling by motor rickshaw to the center of Delhi that day and were unaware of the assassination. As we passed the All India Medical Institute hospital we noticed a huge crowd on the street, growing larger by the moment. By the time we reached the center of the city, shopkeepers were pulling down hard metal shutters over storefronts to protect them from looting by rioters.

News sheets were being passed out on the street to inform shocked crowds that Indira Ghandi had been shot. Unbeknownst to us we had just driven by the very hospital where her body had been taken, in an attempt to save her.

Dave and I realized that we needed to head straight back to our apartment, right behind the All India Medical Institute. We felt we would be safe there for the night even though our own neighborhood was predominantly Sikh.

Sikhism is actually the world's fifth-largest organized religion, with about 25 million followers. India claims the largest population, with about 22 million. Unlike Hindus they believe in only one god, and in the equality of men and women, but like Hindus believe in reincarnation. Sikh men are easy to identify because they usually wear unshaven beards with a turban to cover their long, uncut hair. Our Sikh neighbors were very friendly, enjoying chats on the street in front of their apartments.

The announcement that the Prime Minister had died from her gunshot wounds set off massive revenge killings between Hindus and Sikhs. Everywhere we looked we saw petrified men and women scurrying to get off the streets and back to the comparative safety of their homes. Riots throughout that night and the next days left more than a thousand innocent Sikhs dead. Indira's son, Rajiv Gandhi, took over as Prime Minister.

It was a terrifying time, to say the least. A time to lean hard on the Prince of Peace.

New OM team members were scheduled to arrive from Europe that first night. I remember our nervousness as we took Barbara Geddes to the airport for her flight home, and picked up new recruits for the Afghan immigrant team.

On the way we shuddered at the sight of a bus that had been torched. Later, as we took a new couple to their accommodation in another suburb of Delhi, we drove by a man driving his car backwards with great speed, keeping up with our car as we moved forward. He was obviously trying to get away from a mob intent on ransacking his car and possibly killing him. That encounter was a bit too close for comfort. At the time I didn't know how to sort my emotions, feeling too numb and horrified by the violence around us.

I do remember that when riots broke out in the city, all of our immediate neighbors wanted to protect each other, regardless of their different religious beliefs. But the anxiety level felt so thick it could be sliced with a knife. Rumors circulated that a mob was going to march on our area. We OMers decided to hold a prayer meeting even as our neighbors gathered bricks and big knives, in case they needed to protect themselves. Thankfully, the mob never showed up.

That night I lay in bed praying about the frightening situation we were trapped in. God told me that it was up to Him if it was my time to die or not, and I should just leave it in His hands. With that assurance settling my heart I was able to fall into a deep sleep. In the morning our Hindu landlord told us his family had hardly slept at all. Although Hindus put their faith in tens of thousands of "gods", none could protect or give peace except Jesus, our Prince of peace.

We went up to the flat roof of our apartment complex where we often hung our clothes to dry, and stood stunned. The city's horizon was filled with smoldering plumes of smoke in all directions. Buses, cars and other vehicles had been destroyed. People had burned to death while locked in their homes. It was a terrible and unforgettable scenario. We were gripped by the somber and surreal evidence of man's hatred to man.

On the third day of the unrest we were scheduled to go to Bombay (now called Mumbai) for leadership meetings. Wayne and Shiela Toews had agreed to stand in for us at the guest house. When we got to the train station for our trip south, however, we found every platform jammed with people trying to escape the city. Wayne helped us to get onto our carriage by lodging his big body in the doorway. We squeezed past under the arm he had braced against the door, only to be met by passengers packed like sardines at the entrance to the carriage.

As I wedged myself through this crowd of mostly men I could feel hands touching me all over my body--rear, crotch and legs. Either they were looking for sexual kicks or my wallet. I felt so violated by their roaming hands I wanted to scream.

When we finally arrived at our ticketed seats we discovered they were already crammed with people who had taken our spots. We didn't know what to do—we scarcely had room to sit down while the other passengers, without tickets, insisted on staying.

Finally the conductor came through to collect tickets and the others left.—Which was when I realized my cashmere shawl was missing. I was very upset that these people had taken advantage of us. I have always hated being stolen-from, it feels like such a violation of space. But God in His kindness later provided another shawl for me when we returned to Delhi. What an initiation for a girl coming from rural Wisconsin, where so few people live in comparison to India's teeming millions! I have had to learn not to let possessions possess me. Only God is the One I should allow to possess me, and me, Him.

I mentioned before that the sheer numbers of people everywhere in India was probably one of the hardest things to get used to, whether we were on streets, shopping in bazaars or travelling in buses. The country was home to over 1.3 billion men, women and children: four times the number we had in the US, although America was three times larger.

One time Dave and I joined the Afghan outreach team to pass out evangelistic tracts about Jesus and His love for all people. We were at a parade near the famous India Gate where many parades took place. There had to have been over a million people at this event. If a stampede took place, we could have been killed. But everyone was so eager to receive our leaflets that they surrounded us like swarms of mosquitos in a swamp. They almost ripped the tracts out of our hands.

A group of young fellows in their 20's surrounded me and started flirting and making rude comments as I handed out literature. At once I stopped and walked away from them, feeling unsafe. I couldn't see Dave or the other workers anywhere. Eventually, however, I did find my team members and husband, and we returned safely to our homes.

Some time later Dave and I traveled alone to predominantly-Muslim Pakistan, to renew our India visa at the border. Our OM van that we traveled in we got from Kathmandu, Nepal on a previous trip. It was so old and about ready to be scrapped. As we got to the Pakistan and Indian border on the western side of Amritsar, where the famous Sikh temple had been blasted by Indira Gandhi's troops, we found out that the van's passport visa had expired. This meant we had to leave the van and go all the way back to Delhi via a night bus. I happened to be having my "monthly" then, too. What a horribly uncomfortable situation. To make matters worse a passenger in the seat behind me tried to grope my buttocks during that long, nighttime ride.

I found it appalling that some men could behave so disgustingly to a lady in their country—or anyone else, for that matter. They seemed to me like unleashed wild dogs taking any opportunity to satisfy their sexual curiosities. The Bible does say that God will let people be driven by their "depraved minds" if they don't adhere to His Word and His healthy, pure and wholesome ways. I am so glad that He understands how we feel when other people invade us in ways that are harmful to our spirits. He is able to help us forgive, and move on.

Once we got to the government center in Delhi we realized the offices were about to close. We only had a short amount of time to get the vehicle passport visa extended, so that we could legally leave India. I remember desperately praying that God would move on our behalf. We ourselves were in India without a visa as well, because at the border crossing--where we had left our vehicle in the impounded vehicle area, no man's land--our India visa had already been canceled in our passports. I was so upset that I told God I was going to give up on walking by faith, because it was just too hard in this part of the world.

But then He told me: *You just watch and see what will happen.* And sure enough, the person who was supposed to stamp our vehicle passport visa stayed to do his job after office hours! I was so amazed. We then went to the Delhi train station and got ourselves some nighttime tickets to return to the border. We were able to cross into Pakistan with all of our belongings, which were still safely inside the van.

God pulls us through in His timing to humble us and show us His power. I definitely saw that I had a heart that needed His

Holy Spirit daily to keep my heart soft so I could live according to His will. Being totally yielded to Him was the only way to peace.

After crossing the barren-looking border we arrived in Lahore, Pakistan's second-largest city, where the OM office was located. A missionary family had left, so we were able to live in their place for a short time. This was preferable to staying at the office's guest room, with no privacy. We were blessed with our own kitchen and living quarters without a lot of guests around like we had had in Delhi. However, the dwelling stood close to a mosque that blasted out a call to prayer five times a day. The early hours in the morning before dawn was what got to me the most. The folks living in the neighborhood were friendly enough, but I was missing the green grass and leafy trees of my home in Wisconsin.

The nation of Pakistan came into being in 1947 when the British Parliament declared it a separate and independent dominion from India. It was to be a "pure land" for Muslims. The "Partition" of Pakistan from India set off one of the largest mass migrations—and bloodbaths--in history, when 14 million Hindus, Sikhs and Muslims suddenly found themselves in the wrong country. Many fled, leaving their belongings behind. Up to two million never made it. Whole trainloads of men, women and children were massacred.

Small wonder that bitterness still haunts these neighboring nations. India and Pakistan have fought three major and one minor war over territorial disputes since 1947. Pakistan was initially at a severe disadvantage, cut off from the financial and military assets of British India. But it has survived, and it has made itself a global center of Islam. 97% of Pakistanis today are Muslims, and mosques are found on almost every street corner.

During our few weeks in the country I noticed many cultural differences from India. Men and women didn't really mix much in social settings and there was absolutely no hand shaking between the two genders. Fewer women were on the streets when I walked along with Dave. Men would sometimes try to touch me in places that were not allowed to be touched by anyone other than a husband. This made me feel unsafe going to shops or anywhere else in public. Especially alone. I was shocked at how men simply stared at me for no apparent reason. Of course I stuck out like a sore thumb, being white-skinned and blue-eyed in a predominantly brown-skinned society--and a woman at that! It didn't seem to matter that I was wearing the Pakistani *shalwar kameez,* to be respectful of their dress code.

Pakistani people really did like to socialize, however, even if it was just in groups of men or groups of women. Many times I saw ladies sitting around with each other when they weren't cooking food for the family, washing clothes by hand or cleaning their houses. The ladies normally wore very colorful headscarves and long tunics over loose trousers. Most of the houses in our neighborhood were apartment buildings with several floors. In the courtyards the children's excited playtimes were accompanied by giggles, squeals, yelling and screaming, just like most normal children hanging out with their friends.

The food was different because everyone in Pakistan enjoyed eating meat while most Indians didn't; the Hindu belief in reincarnation made gods of many animals. Dave and I took advantage of the meaty meals while we stayed in Lahore.

During those weeks we set about preparing an evangelistic trek up in the mountains just north of Islamabad, the capital city of Pakistan. The area we were focusing on was close to the southern border of China. We wanted to hand out gospel literature and simple medicines to relieve people's sickness in this remote area. After making beef jerky and other salty snack items from scratch we decided to make a quick trip to Peshawar via bus to visit with Gordon and Grace Magney and borrow their hiking gear.

The Magneys lived in Rahatabad, just outside the city of Peshawar. They had settled there after being pushed out of Afghanistan when the Russians invaded, starting a humanitarian work to assist Afghan refugees as they flooded over the border, Not only did they offer practical aid like blankets, food and clothing, but solar cookers that allowed displaced people to cook their food in the camps where wood, coal and keresene fuel was scarce. Later on, after serving the Afghans faithfully for many years in Peshawar, they were able to return to Kabul, Afghanistan's capital, to assist war victims. Gordon gave us valuable advice about our proposed trekking trip and generously lent us the hiking gear we needed.

Finally we had everything together to fly up to the mountainous town of Gilgit in the lower part of the Hunza valley. Dave and I met up with our other two teammates for the trek in the Islamabad airport. Chris Thompson was an American and Mickey Able was a Pakistani brother. After we flew into Gilgit we paid a jeep owner to take us on to within a few villages from the Chinese border. The mountainous region of Hunza was spectacular; enough to take our breath away.

The driver tied a goat to the side of our jeep and stuffed two chickens under the back seat. Three of us sat in the rear and two were in front. After hours on the narrow mountain road we were relieved to finally reach our destination and climb out of the jeep. When the driver reached under the seat to pull out the chickens he found them dead and stiff as a board. I'm not sure if they gave up after being squished by the three of us in back or if they just died of fright and lack of air. Since they hadn't been dead long I hoped that people could still use the meat. Chicken is a rare delicacy in that part of the world. As for the goat, he was still in great shape at the end of the trip!

We had an interesting time over the next three adventurous weeks, walking from village to village handing out literature about Jesus' love, along with much-needed medicines. When we prayed with people it was amazing to see how open they were to new ideas outside their habitual way of thinking.

One evening on the trek, while eating at one of the simple hostels where we stayed overnight, we met a young man who told us he was a secret believer in Christ. He shared this confidence in a low voice for fear of local people hearing him. At that time I didn't realize how dangerous discovery would have been for him; certainly it would have led to persecution and rejection by his society. The fact that we never saw this fellow again has always bothered me. I hope he was encouraged by our encounter. Looking back, I am still deeply impressed that he had the courage to let us know about his faith. This young man like many others who chose Jesus' way would have a challenging road ahead.

After returning to Lahore we had only a short time before heading back to finish our commitment with OM India. We stayed in Delhi for several more months, running the hospitality house and sharing the love of Jesus with the poor. Then in the late fall of 1984 we returned to the States for a furlough. God had kept His hand on us throughout our journeys in the subcontinent. We looked forward to the next assignment He had for us!

CHAPTER 4

Muslim Neighbors & Motherhood: Leaning on God

Dave and I knew that God wanted us to remain in global work for the rest of our lives. In the last few years we had changed a lot and matured in our faith. Exposure to extreme poverty had broadened my farm girl's perspective; I was now aware there were far more needy people in the world than those we saw in the United States.

For several months during our furlough we visited churches to share what God was doing in India and Pakistan. We always ended by challenging our audiences with the fact that God wanted more people involved whether by praying, giving financially, going themselves or sending workers to the field.

Then OM contacted us with another proposition. Bangladesh leaders Roger and Jackie Adkins were taking a study leave. Would we consider stepping in during their absence to help facilitate the discipleship and evangelistic programs in that country? After thought and prayer, we said yes.

Bangladesh was originally called East Pakistan, part of the Partition of 1947 that allocated a separate land for Muslims. Located far from Pakistan proper to the east of India, however, the peoples' demands to become a country of their own eventually led to independence in 1971.

We flew to the Bangladesh capital city of Dhaka in January 1986. Our new home was a very simple, tin-roofed dwelling that had formerly been used as servants' quarters. The place boasted a grass-thatched porch covering, but no air conditioning at all. I hadn't grown up with AC and Wisconsin summer temperatures could range from 75-115 degrees Fahrenheit, although the humidity varied. The subtropical heat of Bangladesh, however, was much more than I bargained for. In addition, summer monsoons brought a long rainy season from June to October.

On the flight to Dhaka from America I came down with strep throat. I felt so sick on the day of arrival that I just wanted to turn around and go home to the USA. Fortunately, a missionary nurse came to see me and gave me antibiotics. She instructed me to rest. Dave had to go on a trip a day or two later so that Roger Adkins could introduce him to the responsibilities he would be taking on. I really wasn't prepared to be left alone in a land I knew nothing about, sick and lonely for my family back in Wisconsin. I admit to feeling totally abandoned.

I stayed with Jackie Adkins in a guestroom at the Young Christian Workers (YCW) base, while Dave visited teams with Roger. She was very kind, and as I continued to recover from the strep throat and rested up, I started to get on board with our new assignment.

Soon after his return Dave and I began taking Bangla language classes. We agreed this was an essential first step in getting us oriented to the new culture. Our daily transport was a three-wheeled bicycle rickshaw, operated by a skinny brown Bengali man. It was a man's world on the streets and I never saw a woman pedaling a rickshaw. It was very hard work. But the women's lot was no easier: females were considered the family baby-makers, clothes-washers (by hand, of course), housecleaners, field workers and food-preparers.

A great many people in Bangladesh were destitute. The country's location on a delta made it prone to natural disasters like floods, cyclones, storm surges, droughts, hurricanes, riverbank erosion and landslides. Although international assistance had considerably reduced the poverty level over the years, it was still one of the poorest nations on earth.

It is also one of the most crowded countries I had ever been in! Only about the size of my own state of Wisconsin, Bangladesh had one of the densest populations worldwide with over 167 million people compared to my state's six million. Most residents were Muslims who believed much differently than I did; differently, too, from the majority of people I had met in India. Now we were living amongst them.

During the two to three months that Dave and I rode to and fro from classes on bicycle rickshaws, we grew used to winding through heavy traffic from other rickshaws and carts drawn by cows; buses and cars blaring their horns; and pedestrians and dogs walking wherever they pleased. I was always glad to get home and off the streets at the end of it. Rickshaws are a great way for their owners to make money, but those little barebones contraptions on wheels are really unsafe amongst all the frantic hustle and bustle of Dhaka's roads.

We started to work at the YCW office, which was another training center of Operation Mobilization located in Mohammadpur, a relatively uncrowded suburb of Dhaka. Today this area is very overpopulated.

The office and training program started after the war, when some young men wanted to help people in Bangladesh find relief physically, emotionally and spiritually. Today, Young Christian Workers is involved in development programs like tailor training for female fistula patients and computer classes and electrical training for men so they can find jobs to sustain themselves and their families. The team is also involved in relief efforts among refugees and disaster victims.

My job at the center was to make sure that our team cook Stuart, a Garo tribal Bengali, prepared healthy meals each day for the young men in training. The menu consisted of rice and curry and large helpings of *dal*—a runny yellow lentil soup.

Dave was in charge of the training, which helped young believers understand what it meant to wholeheartedly follow Jesus by faith. It was actually a discipleship program. Dave was also responsible for writing up stories of how God was using our teams to reach out to the poor and show His great love for them.

After we led the ministry for the agreed time frame, we agreed to stay on for another year because Roger and Jackie Adkins's family were not yet ready to return to the field. God confirmed to Dave and me that this was where He wanted us to serve for the time being.

Bangladesh had a wonderful, green climate all year round. The coldest it got was around 45 degrees F, so it was nothing like Wisconsin winters with its harsh, below-zero temperatures. Palm trees and tropical fruit trees flourished in the countryside, as did rice paddies. In the north, towards the Indian border, there were many tea gardens. The people of Bangladesh loved their rice, wheat and tea.

Within the first few months of language classes we were doing very well getting around Dhaka on bicycle rickshaws, shopping in the bazaars, making friends with team members and stretching our Bengali languages skills. Bangladesh was 89% Muslim so mosques abounded everywhere. Our former assignment in Pakistan helped us get acclimatized to the culture. We loved making friends with people we met.

After about the second month of classes, however, I started feeling a little unwell. I realized I was pregnant with our first baby! While thrilled about this exciting development, I felt frustrated at being so uncomfortable with morning sickness and dysentery while we were still settling in. But I persevered.

Dave and I decided to attend birthing classes that some American missionaries were holding at their house. I found it very valuable to understand what my body was going through with all the hormonal changes--especially since I didn't have access to my mom. Phoning, skyping and email weren't available those days, though of course I wrote to her via "snail mail."

As my pregnancy advanced I fell into a depression, wishing I could quit and go home to my family farm. I was sick and tired of being sick and tired, so far away from everything familiar.

Mike and Elsie Lyth, our area directors, reached out to give me some good advice. The Lyths were two of the pioneers of the YCW work. Mike was from England and Elsie was from the USA and they had three lovely children. Another baby was on the way, although the Lyths were abruptly forced to leave the country before it was born.

Mike told me not to look at the problems that I was facing all at once, because they would seem overwhelming. He suggested a picture for me to think about. I was to look at my difficulties as if they were three mountains. In order to conquer one mountain I only needed to climb that one first. I could only take one step at a time and get over one mountain at a time, not all three at once.

I had to learn that when we have problems that seem unsurmountable, I should only try to solve one before going on to the next. I am so grateful for this simple example of how to tackle life's hurdles. I love challenges, but sometimes they can make us feel overburdened. One step at a time is the best way forward.

My stomach was extra sensitive to oils during my pregnancy, so I needed to be careful of what I chose to eat. This was a big difficulty when every Bengali saturates their food with oil to make it tastier.

Elsie gave me cooking lessons so I could learn to prepare meals with very little oil. Since she, too, was pregnant with her fourth child she proved an excellent coach on teaching me to be a mother. She had such a positive attitude about handling her children, including home-schooling them while carrying the next one.

How good of God to show me His grace during this period by putting such a godly couple into our lives! Even though we were so far away from our own families, and I missed my mom's good advice, our Father provided friends to help parent us as we learned how to be new parents. He knows how to meet our needs whenever we need help.

On the other side of our team house facilities lived another missionary couple, Janet and Jim, with a mission called SIM. I also visited this wife for advice on getting ready for parenthood. I only had to walk out the gate of our walled-in facility, take a left and go down the road about one hundred feet. Janet had extra baby clothes that she was able to lend me during the early days of

Pam - around 5 years old

**Kickapoo Valley
and family farm**

**Pam - holding her
birthday cake**

Pam, Mom, Dad, Gail and Kally

Pam and Dave married -
October 23, 1982

**Dave and Pam
College days1982**

**Kickapoo Valley - Fall
colors from farm house**

**In Delhi
around 1982-1983**

**Guests who came to our
apartment in Delhi for a bit**

Our Church fellowship in our neighborhood

**Our OM van
when we lived in Delhi**

Bangladesh

**Visiting village in
Bangladesh with Rachel**

**Dave, Pam and Rachel
in front of our humble
abode in Bangladesh**

**Dave and I visited Cox
Bazaar at the shore of
the Bay of Bengal**

Dave with YCW team

My sister-in-laws were visiting us in Pakistan

Cuddling Justin while at Wheaton College

I am riding my horse on Dad's farm, 2019

My sister Kally and I watering our horses in the Kickapoo River that our farm borders

Justin was born in USA after we returned

As a family, visited
Peshawar from
Tajikistan

Our first spring in
Tajikistan, 1993

As a family, visited a
village in the mountains

As a family, visited
Romit Valley in
Tajikistan

Relief work in war torn Tajikistan

Pam with the ladies that helped in our house

Riding horses together in Hisor region, Tajikistan

A beautiful painting of a small mosque

Pam traveling in northern Afghanistan

Dave visiting a village in Afghanistan

Playing games at a CADA staff picnic in Warzob Valley

In front of the Botanical Garden entrance in Dushanbe

Nepal

Visited Nepal after Rachel was born

Visited Nepal again when Rachel was older

With Dave's parents and sister Becky in Nepal just outside Kathmandu

our baby's growth. Giving me this neighbor was another example of God's faithfulness.

We attended SIM prayer meetings at Janet and Jim's house quite often. Though the fellowship was mainly for foreigners, that was okay. I always looked forward to praying together and exchanging news. Our YCW team, both foreigners and Bengalis, also held excellent prayer meetings.

One thing I have learned through the years of following God is that He always brings the right people into our lives, just at the right time. Our Father will never leave us or forsake us. He tenderly helps us out with whatever we are facing.

As fall rolled in, the hot temperatures settled down to more comfortable levels. But clouds of dust in the air settled over the city of Dhaka and filtered into our houses. No matter how much I tried to keep our humble abode clean, a new layer of dust appeared every day. But that did not stop me from continuing to get our little place ready for the arrival of our baby. I very much enjoyed the prospect of a new addition to our family!

At the beginning of my ninth month of pregnancy, in December 1986, Dave and I flew three hundred miles southeast to a hospital in the jungle area of Cox's Bazaar, which bordered Myanmar. The hospital had been pioneered by missionaries many years before, just after the civil war when Bangladesh gained it's independence from Pakistan. Dr. Viggo Olsen and others who founded the facility wanted to care for Christian workers so that they would not lose so many to sickness. They also helped many Bengalis in the area, both physically and spiritually. By the time we went to Malamghat Hospital (also called Memorial Christian Hospital) to deliver our baby, it had been around for about twenty years.

Dave escorted me to a guesthouse in the hospital complex, set in a beautiful forest overlooking a tidal stream from the Bay of Bengal. We didn't know how long it would be before our daughter would be born. It was close to Christmas and one could feel the joy in the air.

Another couple who had attended Bangla language classes with us in Dhaka happened to be at the hospital at the same time. I was glad to have them as neighbors in the guest house as we both waited for our babies to be born.

Dave returned to Dhaka briefly to keep up with YCW administration work. I stayed in the jungle guest house for about week without him, not very happy about being left alone in this unfamiliar situation—especially as there was no way to keep in contact with each other.

Looking back now, I know I felt resentment that he had abandoned me when it wasn't absolutely necessary. Of course, there were loving people around me including the hospital staff, so I wasn't totally alone. I thanked God for His faithful commitment to me, even when family members weren't nearby.

Dave returned to the hospital just before Christmas. Our baby hadn't yet arrived, and the waiting was not easy. We celebrated Jesus' birth with the Baptist missionaries and had a beautiful time singing familiar songs and eating lots of good food. The fellowship was sweet. It was certainly a far cry from the way we celebrated Christmas back home, in the cold and snow! Though it was the cool season in Bangladesh, snow was of course unheard of.

Eventually on January 1st, two weeks after my due date, our daughter Rachel Ingralisa Lovett made her entrance into the world. An American doctor and nurse took care of the delivery, along with a Bengali midwife. My labor from the time the waters broke until Rachel was born lasted 26 hours. It wasn't an easy birth, but worth all the effort. We were so glad to have our baby join us out in "the middle of nowhere" on the first day of a new year. Rachel brought us so much joy!

We stayed for about one more week in Coxe's Bazaar before we flew back to Dhaka and our little home in Mohammadpur. I wore an elegant blue saree onto the small plane that took us to Chittagong for the first lap, to pick up more passengers. When I finished nursing Rachel she decided it was time to make her presence felt. Her bowel movement went all over my lovely saree. I got off the plane in Chittagong, leaving Dave to hold our daughter while I made a beeline towards the bathroom to wash off the mess. This was my initiation to motherhood in the "be ready for anything" traveling mode!

When I reboarded the plane all went well. Rachel spared me a second explosion during the flight, thank goodness. Arriving back in the Young Christian Workers base, we found that the Bengali brothers on our team had hung a wonderful "welcome back" sign on our quarters. The sign was decorated in bright colors, and we were truly touched by this expression of love towards us and our new little daughter.

After we settled back into our tin-roofed home I started to unpack the packages of baby clothes and diapers that Dave's mom and dad had sent to us via post. The precious baby things for Rachel arrived in perfect condition, and the timing was also perfect. Unfortunately we were forced to pay a pretty penny for customs to release the boxes to us.

A few days later and still readjusting to base life, Dave and I ate supper in our dining area, across the yard from our main bedroom. We had Rachel with us because she was awake and fussing. When we suddenly heard a sound like rain outside our door I thought at first the garden helper was watering the garden. But when I opened the door of our dining area I was shocked to see the other side of the housing unit ablaze. Huge flames licked out of the building. I couldn't believe my eyes. I yelled to Dave that there was a fire.

Dave immediately ran into the burning house to try to put out the fire while I ran to the other side of the compound, where the YCW team brothers were living, and shouted the Bengali word "*Agoon!*" "*Agoon!*" "*Agoon!*" which I had just learned meant "fire." Little did I expect to use this word so soon after learning it! God in His mercy spared the place from total destruction that evening.

Most of all we were grateful that we had taken little Rachel with us when we went to eat. I shudder to think how she might have been burned inside our grass-thatched bedroom.

It is so important to keep an "attitude of gratitude" at all times! Complaining is one of my weaknesses, but I have learned the hard way over all these years that it zaps our energy. When we count our blessings it is life-giving, emotionally and relationally.

Our co-workers Mike and Elsie Lyth had to go to Nepal to live because the Bengali government didn't keep their commitment to their visa allotment. We decided to visit Kathamndu with Rachel to attend a conference and to say our hellos and goodbyes to the Lyth's who had encouraged us greatly while living in Bangladesh that first year. Kathmandu was surrounded by beautiful mountains.

Rachel continued to grow fast in her first year of life. Caring for her was a big learning curve for Dave and I. We had to resist getting swallowed up by the ministries abounding around us: discipling the young men that were part of the YCW leadership development program, and evangelistic outreaches.

We enjoyed being new parents, although I often wished for my mom's wise counsel. I was thankful that the other missionaries around me had more experience in raising kids in a tropical culture and climate. They gave me all kinds of advice—whether I asked for it or not!

After our two year commitment was finished in Bangladesh we returned to the States. Rachel was around eleven months old by then. We had learned a lot while living in such a unique environment and we cherished the many friends that we had made. All the same, I secretly hoped God wouldn't ask us to return there permanently, because I had struggled so much with sickness. But I have returned to Bangladesh several times in past years to encourage friends who continue reaching out to others.

Dave and I sought God's plan for the next chapter and after a short break in New Jersey and Wisconsin we did return to the mission field. This time we moved to Peshawar, Pakistan, to become friends with Afghan refugees.

CHAPTER 5

Living on a Knife Edge

Before leaving Bangladesh, we had already discussed moving to Pakistan when we returned to Asia. We felt God was calling us to live in Peshawar, near the Afghan border, so we could get involved in reaching out to Afghan refugees. Peshawar was a border city that made sense for Afghans escaping the raging war against Russians in their homeland. Many of the refugees passed through the Khyber Pass that ended ten miles west of Peshawar. Over three million men, women and children were crammed into camps along the border of Afghanistan/Pakistan in the Khyber region and other parts of Pakistan. About 100,000 lived within Peshawar's city limits. Small wonder the place was called "little Kabul"! Dozens of relief agencies worked in the area to provide emergency food, medical help, tents, blankets, clothing and water to these desperate people. Other groups built latrines or supplied solar-operated cooking stoves. Yet these efforts seemed like a drop in a bucket when dealing with such a massive humanitarian crisis.

While we were in the States one of our co-workers from Malaysia, Lim Seng Watt, finished his two year work commitment in Bangladesh. He agreed to collect our few belongings in Dhaka and drive them across the border to India, then on to Pakistan. That way when we arrived in Peshawar a few months later, some of our things would be waiting for us.

Meanwhile Dave, eleven-month-old Rachel and I completed our short but busy furlough. It was a thrill to show off our little bundle of joy to all our family and friends who hadn't yet seen her. Rachel enjoyed meeting everyone, even though she was so small. As we traveled around the states from the east coast to the Midwest, down to Texas and back to New Jersey, we visited sponsors, relatives and churches to let them know what had been happening in our lives and how God was at work in Muslim lands.

All too soon it was time to say goodbye again. Rachel had reached the age of one and a half years and it was much harder this time to leave our families behind. Now that I am in the grandparent stage of life myself I realize that leave-taking wasn't hard only for us, it was a grief for our parents.

The journey to Pakistan was the longest we'd ever undertaken. After flying many hours from New Jersey to California and then on to Manila in the Philippines, we continued finally to Karachi and then on to Islamabad. From the airport we had a five hour bus trip west to Peshawar City, located in the northwest frontier near the famous Khyber Pass. We were totally exhausted when we finally collapsed in Gordon and Grace Magney's house in Rahatabad, just outside Peshawar. By the grace of God our precious toddler, Rachel Ingralisa Lovett, survived crossing all of those time zones, with no ill effects. But needless to say we never traveled to the subcontinent that way again! The reason we chose that route was to allow a stop-off in California, so that I could see my cousin and her family who were also in ministry, her husband serving at Bethel Church in Redding.

In Peshawar we lived at first with the Magneys and started right away to take Dari language lessons. We knew this would make getting around the city easier, and help us make friends with the Afghan refugees around us. While learning a new language wasn't easy after learning Bengali, we felt it was an essential step towards ministering to local people.

In order to take the Dari language course we had to take public transport from Rahatabad to University Town where the course was being offered to foreigners. Dave watched Rachel when I went off to my classes, which meant walking alone through the hot, dusty neighborhood to the main road, where I caught a small minivan and traveled four or five miles further. I was so nervous going on my own. Having grown up in the country I never had to take public transport to get anywhere in Wisconsin, unless I was catching a Greyhound bus to visit a major city. So this kind of travel in Peshawar was a challenge.

When it was Dave's turn to attend classes I took care of Rachel at the Magney's spacious house, which had a walled-in, beautiful yard surrounding it. While we were very grateful for the Magney's kindness in hosting us, the situation wasn't ideal because Rachel had no other children to play with. I remember occupying her as well as I could by having her help me with chores. We made a game of washing clothes and hanging them up to dry, cleaning our rooms, and so forth.

Eventually we were able to move out of Gordon and Grace's house and into our own little place, in a suburb called Shaheen Town. Many Afghans lived in this community amongst their Pushtun Pakistani neighbors. We moved into the rented house so quickly we didn't even have time to paint it. The place was large but dark and dingy, with cement floors and a mud-packed roof to keep it cooler in the scorching summer heat. Fortunately we also had one air conditioner to help lower the temperature when it soared above 110 degrees Fahrenheit.

Dave's sister Becky, who had been working in India for a short time with the same organization as us, transferred to Peshawar in 1989. She and her friend Megan from Australia moved into the back rooms of our house. Both were with a non-governmental agency called SERVE, started by Gordon Magney to help destitute Afghan refugees.

It was so nice to have friends sharing our big house. Rachel roamed around the place like a little princess. We needed to employ a guard, though, because living in Peshawar wasn't exactly safe. Seven fundamentalist political Mujahideen (freedom fighter) groups were based in Peshawar, loosely united under Islam with the goal of controlling the possible new Afghan government, after the Russians left. Up to 35,000 Arab and other foreign fighters had also gravitated to the area to fight, forming the core of what later became Al-Qaeda.

Gulbuddin Hekmatyar was one of the Mujahideen leaders of a group called Hezb-e-Islami. His followers intimidated people into becoming what they considered "good Muslims." Their militant enforcement of Sharia or Islamic law was a reign of terror amongst the population. Living in the midst of all these Islamic extremists, who eventually formed both the Taliban and the Al-Qaeda movements, was not a comfortable situation.

Immediately next door to us was a home for small boys. Their proximity called for getting a dog to discourage the children from constantly climbing over the walls and invading our yard. The boys didn't understand boundaries at all, so many times they poked their heads up over the wall to talk with us or just stare, because they thought we foreigners looked so different from them.

Sometime during the first year we hired an Afghan Pamiri cook to help with the shopping, cooking, house cleaning and clothes ironing. Studying the Dari language, adjusting to the new culture and raising Rachel was about all I could handle. The Dari language was very different from the Bengali language grammar structure that I had learned before. Of course, most of the vocabulary was very different, too. I remember one time we went back to Bangladesh to see old friends and used Bengali to talk with them. When we returned to Pakistan I spoke to the cook who was helping in our kitchen. He looked at me very strangely. At first I couldn't figure out why, but then it dawned on me that I was using the Bengali language instead of the Dari I was learning. We both laughed hard because he thought I was speaking jibberish. I had to remember to just stick with Dari and not mix Bengali with it, even though a few words were the same.

On that same trip we had visited with Dave's parents and his sister Becky who was living in Kathmandu at that time. It was nice to be surrounded by beautiful snow capped mountains. Gazing upon Mount Everest one day was quite spectacular because it was such a clear day. We enjoyed the family time with Rachel's grandparents and aunt Becky.

Eventually, since our daughter still had few other children to play with, we decided to send her to a Christian pre-school. Started by missionaries, the school was only about a seven minute drive from our house. When she came home she took a nap and then enjoyed free reign on the sidewalk next to our house's hard mud yard, riding her plastic push truck. We made sure she had plenty of arts and craft activities as well as toys to keep her busy.

By our first Christmas we were attending an English-speaking international church. Although there were Pakistani churches in the area, the services were in the Urdu language. There were no Afghan churches at all. We enjoyed gathering with about seventy five people from Germany, America, Australia, Switzerland, Malaysia, Singapore, Canada and many other countries for worship. Dave, Rachel and I participated in a Christmas play and I took the part of Mary while Dave played Joseph and Rachel represented the baby Jesus. Practice for this drama started in the month of November and we took it seriously.

This nativity play turned out to be a great way to share Jesus with Afghan refugees, most of whom had no idea of what Christmas was all about. The drama was staged outdoors in a nearby church compound, and as our Afghan and Pakistani guests passed through the gate they stacked their rifles and other weapons in the place provided for them. Then they sat down on rows of chairs set up in the spacious though crowded churchyard. These men, women and children were in such desperate need of hearing God's good news about Jesus' birth! They had suffered horrific traumas from the war that only the Prince of Peace could heal. Our audience seemed happy to hear the good news of Jesus, and took away loads of resources from the welcome table displayed that evening.

Although we lived in a hot, dry frontier city, we made sure that we had a Christmas tree that year. If I remember right we bought a potted cedar tree in a meagerly-filled plant bazaar. Though the decorations were sparse, we loved that tree. One evening our team gathered in Gordon and Grace's house to sing carols and share treats. It was a great time of celebration as we workers from around the globe sang our hearts out.

Although we made Pakistani friends, we continued to concentrate on learning Afghan Dari instead of the Pakistani language of Urdu. Our main focus was building friendships with refugees so we could be an encouragement to them.

As time went by, we established a relationship with two Afghan single fellows. They came to our house for Bible studies once a week with Dave. Anxious to respect their culture which segregated men and women, my job was to get the tea and sweets ready for Dave to serve our visitors in the front room. This room was quite spacious with a gray cement floor and carpet in the center. We had it furnished with traditional wooden decorative brown chairs shaped like little thrones, with cushions on them. I had never seen chairs like those in the West.

I kept Rachel entertained so that Dave wasn't distracted from answering any questions our new friends had about the Bible, Jesus and faith. Slowly, they began to understand who Jesus Christ really was. We were thrilled when the day came that they prayed with Dave and opened their hearts to our living, loving God, putting their trust in His Son.

In order to protect the privacy of Afghans who were seekers, we never hosted a study when the cook and guard were at our house. We gave each of them Bibles and other Christian materials to read on their own. Our prayer for each person was that God would open their eyes, so they could experience His love for themselves.

Dave was a fulltime Persian language student at the University. This allowed us to befriend Afghan refugees and also to practice our new Dari language skills. We visited the camps once or twice, but many refugees were able to rent cheap housing units in the city. The dwellings in the camps were made of mud and makeshift roofs while the units in Peshawar had more comforts like private toilets, showers, kitchenettes, electricity and locks on their doors.

One family we visited quite often told us that in Afghanistan they had had to hide next to a cliff while Russian military helicopters used searchlights to pinpoint would-be refugees. The family was very frightened, and grateful to have escaped with their lives.

Another person, one of my Dari tutors, told me about her father who had suffered torture from the Russians. They had tried to extract information by pulling out his fingernails. The pain was excruciating. She told me that it was hard to trust anyone, because you never knew who was a spy.

From our years on the field we knew it was essential for our family to make time for relaxation and recreation together. The constant tension of the very conservative culture we lived in took its toll. We liked to go for walks in parks—though they were never as lushly green as those back home--and enjoyed swimming at an international hotel in the city. During our years in Peshawar I took Rachel swimming quite often with other foreign mothers and children, at a pool owned by the Pearl Continental Hotel. The five star hotel was about twenty-five minutes' drive from our house, and a great challenge to negotiate since the roads were crowded and littered. Pedestrians often crossed carelessly right in front of the car. I really dreaded the thought of an accident on those roads, filled with male Muslim drivers. Female drivers were definitely in the minority.

Once we made it to the pool in a sweat we were more than ready to jump into the water. It was a comical scenario because we women entered the hotel covered head to toe in our long, flowing outfits, called *chadors*. As soon as we got to the swimming pool locker room we changed into our swimsuits, leaving us in what would be considered a naked state according to the local Muslim dress code. Both Christian and Muslim women were required to cover themselves completely on the streets, even wearing scarves over their hair. The more religious veiled their faces, as well.

As a foreign woman with blue eyes driving on the crowded streets, as a passenger in a public minivan or riding in the back of a horse-drawn, two-wheeled cart or just walking--I found that I was stared at a lot. Men tried to get my attention to talk or shame me with their words or eyes. I needed to be very strict in how I presented myself. I forced myself not to be friendly, although I am normally a very outgoing person. I needed to repress that part of my personality while out and about in public.

One of my language tutors covered her face completely, except for her nose and eyes. Other women wore a tentlike covering over their outfits called a *burka*, hiding their whole body from the top of their heads to the bottom of their ankles. Only a mesh screen at eye level allowed them to see anything. As you can imagine, wearing cloaks like these was suffocating in Peshawar's extreme heat. I heard that some women carried little straight pins or safety pins, ready to poke a man if he touched her body wrongly. This was one way to protect themselves! The key was to never look a man directly in the eyes while out in public.

I often thought how unfair it was that women so often took the blame for unacceptable behavior in conservative societies. Unthinkable as it is, thousands of Muslim, Hindu and Christian women have become the victims of acid attacks by men who want to punish them for what they perceive as disobedience or immodesty. Many have lost their eyesight and remain horribly disfigured for the rest of their lives. Although such attacks have decreased through new legislation, enforcement of protective laws is not consistent.

Whenever Rachel and I went to visit other people, we dressed carefully. I didn't always drive a car in Peshawar, so we were often exposed to the hustle and bustle on the streets. As we picked our way past mud-brick, walled-in homes and small businesses, throngs of pedestrians brushed past us. Some were fully veiled women, their burkas flowing in the wind.

In the open market, buyers struck bargains with sellers over the price of chickens, kebabs on skewers, car tires, carved wooden furniture, and a myriad other items. Sometimes we took two-wheeled, horse drawn wagons, called "tongas". I instructed Rachel not to look into people's eyes as we sat on the back bench of the wagon. This was much nicer riding than walking to our destinations, especially when the hard, clay-dirt alleys turned to mud underfoot after a rain.

In August 1989, another of Dave's sisters from New Jersey, Sue Lovett, came out to visit us in Peshawar. Becky was already living with us in our rented house, so the two shared a room in the back part of the house. Megan had left by that time.

During Sue's visit the five of us went on a five hour trip to the hill station of Murree, Pakistan. The town, located in the outer Himalayas, has been a favorite tourist destination since the 1850's. We rented a little mountainside cabin and enjoyed a small break from the heat. I was so happy that we could all be together in that lovely, cool climate, and that Rachel could have such a nice change of environment.

Our "princess" was a tough little girl who always wanted to be in charge. One day, I remember, Sue and Becky knocked on our bedroom door. Before Dave or I could answer, Rachel yelled, "Come on in, girls!" I didn't have to wonder where her bossy disposition came from.

One of the highlights of our relaxing vacation was going horseback riding. This was a rare treat for me since I missed horses and riding so much. The owners of the horses walked or ran alongside of us, supposedly to ensure we had no accidents. I sat little Rachel in front of me, in the same saddle. All was well until I decided to canter my horse. The animal unfortunately had an unsafe snaffle bit in its mouth and was soon running out of control. I was scared to death that he wasn't going to stop, but in the end the owner got him reined in. I didn't try that again! I was so afraid that Rachel and I were going to end up on the ground, in pieces.

Later on, towards the end of the week, we took a simple hiking trail that led to a rocky overlook. The view was stunning. Rachel stood next to me, unafraid of heights. Below we could see the American international boarding school; I knew many foreign children attended this facility while their parents worked in Pakistan or neighboring countries.

On our way back to Peshawar we dropped Sue off at the Islamabad airport for her flight back to the United States. We were sad to see "Aunt Sue" leave, but felt grateful for the great time we all had together in our mountain retreat.

Not long after our return to our home in Shaheen Town, I started feeling quite sick to my stomach. I went for a pregnancy test and--lo and behold--I was already one month pregnant with our second child. I was so happy to be carrying another baby, a son whom we later named Justin Michael Lovett. However, I did not anticipate how miserable I would become over the next months.

I had regular monthly checkups with a Salvation Army missionary midwife, but along with morning sickness I was repeatedly assaulted with bouts of dysentery. No matter how careful I was I kept picking up parasites as I visited people in their homes. Contamination could have come from our own kitchen as well, since we were not very diligent about keeping a high standard of hygiene. Maybe the problem was from the grapes that I craved all the time. I don't know, but it seemed like I kept getting sick almost daily with dysentery in addition to severe morning sickness.

It was a very depressing state of affairs. When a show of blood during the mid-trimester warned us of the danger of a possible miscarriage, I was told to rest a lot. We were so afraid of losing the baby.

Meanwhile the stress of our days escalated as Peshawar became increasingly unstable. Russian control of Afghanistan was overthrown in 1989, leaving 1.5 million dead and millions of others uprooted. But that war-ravaged country was now locked in a civil war headed by Afghan mujahideen warlords. The violence had spilled into Peshawar. Foreigners were being threatened by mujahideen leader Gulbuddin Hekmatyar's radical Islamic faction. It was like living on a knife edge.

And then, in the winter of 1989, one of our co-workers went missing.

Dave, Rachel and I had visited our Canadian friend only the night before. We wanted to say goodbye before Tom flew the next day to join his wife and two sons, who had already left Pakistan. He was packing up many of their household belongings to take with him, and getting other items together to sell or give away.

I remember that on that cold, eerie, dark night we invited him over to our house for a last meal together. He declined, explaining that he had been invited to another home that evening. I didn't understand why I felt such an evil presence surrounding us as we said our final goodbyes to Tom on the street. I shrugged away the premonition as we walked from his house and headed back to our neighborhood a short distance away.

A day or two later we attended an English service at the international church. When someone stood to announce that our co-worker had not shown up at the office the day after we saw him, I shuddered deep within myself. Tom was the husband of one of my good friends, the father of the boys Rachel had played with at least once a week. Rosanne and I often sat around watching them, talking about all kinds of life issues. And now, tragically, Tom was gone.

To think we were the last to see him, on the night before he was kidnapped! I felt fear grip me deep inside.

The next days and weeks were a sad and shocking time for everyone as Dave and several colleagues began undercover investigations. They tried to learn if any neighbors or store owners in the area had seen or heard anything about Tom's whereabouts. The local police were also involved in the investigations.

Once during this terrible time Dave reported that while he was walking down the busy alleyway called Chicken Street, in Shaheen Town, one of our Pushtun acquaintances had ridden past him on his bicycle. Dave saw the man lift his hand and draw it across his throat, as if it was a knife. It was obviously a warning: Dave must stop asking questions about our missing co-worker.

This incident made me more apprehensive than ever about continuing to live in Shaheen Town. The Islamic fundamental organizations definitely had representatives living not too far from our house. Hekmatyar Gulbuddin's men even had "hanging houses" in parts of the city, where people they decided weren't good enough Muslims were strangled to death or tortured. As we made our way around the city via mini buses, cars, horse drawn *tongas* or walking, we noticed many men carrying machine guns on their shoulders. No wonder we always felt an ugly tension in the air, despite the friendly hospitality that most people showed us.

One day we were on our way home from the international church in Peshawar. Only minutes after we passed a particular turnoff from the busy street, some people were blown up by a car bomb. To know that we narrowly missed that carnage made me feel terribly unsafe. It was practically impossible to carry on with our normal lives. I just wanted to leave Pakistan, especially now that I was pregnant and constantly sick.

When someone asked Rachel what her mom was like during this time, she pretended to puke into a pail. This picture was all too accurate! One medical professional said that I had gastroenteritis, but whenever I had a stool test it always showed positive for parasites. At least seven times in my nine month pregnancy I was prescribed low doses of metronidazole, which was not good for a developing fetus. But God kept our baby healthy. I didn't feel I was being a very strong mother for my little girl. Rachel was growing up so fast in a very frightening atmosphere. I wish now I had been more emotionally available to Rachel. But I was barely surviving myself, constantly on edge because of the violence around us. Depressed and unwell, I slept a lot. Thankfully, Dave was a great dad to Rachel and was there for both of us.

Before our second Christmas, Dave's mom and dad, Anne and Bill Lovett, came to visit us in Peshawar, staying in our home. By this time Becky had moved out and gone back to India to work and visit her boyfriend, Mark Pickett from the UK. Their relationship was serious and Mark hoped to persuade Becky to become his wife.

It was great having Dave's parents with us. I did my best to make them feel welcome and tried to prepare a turkey for our Christmas dinner. Unfortunately my oven didn't have a thermostat valve so the bird came out a bit tough and dry, though palatable.

Rachel enjoyed having her grandparents around to entertain her. We attended different Christmas events including an international get together. I remember thoroughly enjoying the homemade rice crispy bars offered on the snack table. I was always trying to keep something in my tummy to fend off morning sickness during my pregnancy. I felt like I had the flu all the time.

I found out years later that Bill and Anne encouraged Dave to take me back to the States, because of my condition. After they left, the midwife at the Salvation Army residence who saw me for prenatal visits also advised me to go home to have the baby. It was obvious I wasn't getting better and she knew I could possibly lose my life, or the baby's.

I was tired of being sick, lonely, angry and scared. Living in Peshawar with the danger of my husband being kidnapped or murdered was the final straw. In late February of 1990 we decided it was time to leave Pakistan and return to the United States.

We packed the house up and sold our possessions to whoever needed them, whether they were Afghans, Pakistanis or expatriates. We were just grateful that someone could use them. Whatever wasn't bought, we let people take away for free. During the last week friends Jeff and Roxanne Johnson opened up their home so the three of us could rest before flying back to the West.

Rachel was three years old at this time and probably had no idea what was really going on. She did know we were going to go visit Grandma and Grandpa, but how much else registered I don't know. Peshawar was a place of upheaval in those days, impacting Pakistanis, Afghans and foreign residents alike. It wasn't until much later that we found out that our colleague *Tom* had been murdered. Another kidnapping was attempted of an American consulate staff member; the man actually broke a limb while managing to escape from his captors. It was a very frightening time, but God was our ever present help.

At the Peshawar airport, when we walked towards the airplane that would fly us to Karachi, we saw it was totally surrounded by armed soldiers carrying automatic weapons. They were stationed there to guard passengers from potential terrorist attacks. For some odd reason this had a calming effect on me, knowing these men would do their jobs diligently.

As the plane lifted off the runway and climbed higher into the air, Dave, Rachel and I said our goodbyes to Peshawar, our home for the last one and one half years. We arrived safely in Karachi, but in the terminal I was so overcome by nausea I had to lie down on a bench. Dave took Rachel with him and went off to check us into our connecting international flight. They left me surrounded by crowds of Pakistani passengers, guarding some of the carry-on bags. I am so thankful that we didn't lose our daughter in the chaos of that Karachi airport! Dave kept his eye on her. More importantly, God had His compassionate hand on all of us, protecting us with His angels.

At last we boarded the flight for New York City and, after several hours in the air, landed in the good old USA. The last leg to Bill and Anne Lovett's house in Berkeley Heights, New Jersey wasn't long. The couple were overjoyed to welcome us, particularly their grandchild, Rachel; and I was delighted simply to fall into bed.

As our family adjusted to the many time zone changes, I didn't at first suffer too much from morning sickness. I was seven months pregnant by this time and dared to hope the nausea was over. But then it started again. I was so very grateful to be in a place where a wide variety of healthy snacks were available, helping to keep the sickness at bay. We all missed our friends in Peshawar, but knew this was where we needed to be for the moment.

Dave's mom and some of our church friends had planned a surprise baby shower for us. I was fast asleep in the bedroom when I heard people starting to arrive at the house. After the shock of our co-worker's kidnapping and months of illness, this outpouring of love from God's people in the States refreshed my soul and spirit. I am still thankful for the thoughtfulness of friends at the First Christian Assembly in Plainfield, New Jersey.

Our daughter Rachel awaited the birth of our second baby with anticipation. She didn't quite understand that she would have to share her mommy and daddy with the little sibling soon to be born!

God provided just the right OBGYN doctor in New Jersey, lined up by our friends. The doctor had been born in Bangladesh and now had his own medical practice in New Providence, New Jersey. I like to joke about God's sense of humor, because our daughter Rachel had been born in Bangladesh at a mission hospital, delivered by an American doctor. Now Justin our son was being born in America at a Catholic hospital, delivered by a Bengali doctor. No one could have arranged this scenario but God. He definitely knows how to provide for us, bless us and show us that He is in control!

After Justin was born on May 15, 1990, we stayed with Dave's parents in Berkeley Heights for a few more weeks, and then began to travel towards the southern part of the States. In Georgia we visited the new Operation Mobilization USA headquarters, wanting to thank the directors and staff for their administrative support while we were on the mission field.

Next, we drove to Texas to see some of my relatives who had lived in San Antonio for years. What a great reunion with my Aunt Judy and Uncle Lawrence Knutson, who had influenced me to get involved in missions by the way they lived. They, too, had been missionaries, serving in the country of Columbia, and we were grateful for their faithful prayers through the years.

At the next stop in Wisconsin, I was so happy to reconnect with my parents on the farm outside of Soldiers Grove. Mom and Dad were especially pleased to see their second grandchild Rachel again and meet Justin for the first time. We had the privilege of riding horses and enjoying the great outdoors. It was wonderful to be back on the farm I had missed so much while living overseas.

Wheaton College, Illinois, was our final stop. Dave had applied to study there for his Master's degree in Cross-cultural Communications, thanks to a scholarship from the Billy Graham Center in Wheaton.

Rachel and Justin made lots of little friends while we lived near other college families that year. Justin grew by leaps and bounds and learned to walk. Rachel kept getting taller, bursting with healthy energy. I was grateful to have recovered my own strength so that I could enjoy being a wife and mother and audit a few classes.

In the spring of 1991, as Dave was finishing up his course, OM's Central Asia Director, Bertil Engqvist, contacted us to ask if we wanted to pioneer a humanitarian work in the country of Tajikistan. After much prayer, consideration and conversation, we decided that this was to be our next step. But we continued to ask God for confirmation, and seek His guidance.

We knew little about Tajikistan, other than it was still suffering greatly from a civil war that had followed seventy years of Soviet rule. We were told that Afghan Dari and the Tajik language were quite similar, and I liked the idea of pioneering a new work in a place with the same language structure of Persian. We had no money, no team and no visa as yet to enter the country. But we thought God was leading us, and stepped out in faith.

We have learned through experience that God provides whenever He leads His people in the direction He wants them to go. We simply need to make ourselves available, and let Him place us where He wants us to be placed.

Then we can befriend people to serve as His lights for those who are living in darkness, without the hope of Christ.

CHAPTER 6

To the Ends of the Earth

It was January of 1993. The prospect of flying over 6500 miles from New York to Tajikistan with two very young children--in the middle of a cold, snowy winter--was daunting. Saying goodbye to our families was even more difficult. We definitely caused our parents heartache by taking their grandchildren to such a far away land. They couldn't even envision what it would be like for us, or when they would see their grandkids again. Rachel had just turned six years old and Justin was two and a half.

A single man, Mike McClelland, traveled with us. We were grateful to have Mike as our first team member since we would be pioneering a whole new project in Dushanbe, the capital of Tajikistan. OM's Development/Humanitarian project was to be called the Central Asian Development Agency (CADA).

Nine hours into our journey it was necessary to change planes at Moscow's international airport. The five of us had to transfer to the domestic airport some distance away in three vans, loaded to the hilt with twenty-six bags. Dave and one of the children were in one van, I went with the other child in the second vehicle and Mike was by himself in the third. On the way we noticed streets lined with huge snowbanks but did not take in much else, we were so completely exhausted by jetlag.

When we arrived at the domestic airport, the drivers with Dave and Mike's help unloaded all of the luggage. Mountains of snow and crisp air surrounded us. Once inside the terminal, we realized that the waiting lounge was barely heated. Not a pleasant discovery. Eventually I realized that I would have to find the children's snow clothes that I had packed in one of the bags. I dug out their boots too, so their little feet wouldn't get cold. I remember being so disappointed by the lack of basic amenities in the waiting area. The international airport, no doubt wanting to make a good impression on foreign visitors, had offered much better facilities. It seemed the domestic terminal was mostly used by locals. The toilets were filthy and smelly. To top it off no toilet paper was supplied. *How could I have brought my kids to this place?* I wanted to scream, but managed to restrain myself.

We got as comfortable as we could in the waiting lounge. Then the airport staff approached to break the news that we could not get on a connecting flight to Dushanbe, because there wasn't any scheduled. That was the last straw. I burst into tears and started to pray for God's deliverance. My idea of deliverance at that point was to get on a plane and head back to New York City, never to return to this inhospitable place. I hated the predicament we were in and, I'm afraid, expressed myself very forcefully.

After Mike, Dave and I lifted the matter to God in prayer and talked further with the airport staff, however, a lady came running up to us. She announced that we could get on a flight to Delhi, India. The pilot was willing to stop on the way and drop us and our twenty-six bags in Dushanbe. What a miracle! God had stepped up to make sure we would arrive, just as He had planned.

Having boarded the Aeroflot plane as a family with Mike, our teammate, we were comforted to think that we had finally embarked on the last leg of our trip. Settling back in our seats we buckled our seat belts, and then proceeded to listen to the stewardess recite the standard take-off safety rules. If I recall, they were in the Russian language, so listening didn't help. The plane taxied to the runway and then began to pick up speed for takeoff.

One thing did seem odd. The stewardesses hadn't bothered to shut the overhead cabin storage compartments. The tarmac was bumpy, so as our speed increased one of our heavy carry-on bags fell out of the overhead hatch onto a passenger's head, then bounced into the aisle. I couldn't help laughing. It was just like one of those hilarious scenes right out of a movie. In retrospect I am sure the poor fellow must have suffered a sore head and neck. Dave was more polite than I was and apologized profusely.

Thank God for laughter, because it alleviated much of the stress I was feeling during this international move with my family.

We finally arrived in Tajikistan, the land that was destined to be our home for the next thirteen years. I was taken aback by the dilapidated conditions of the dingy, gray, Dushanbe airport. But we had safely landed, and so had our multiple bags of belongings so necessary in setting up a home and humanitarian office.

Soon we found ourselves in another comical situation. We were instructed to go through the baggage hole to get inside the terminal! I assume the airport staff assigned to help foreigners enter the country were not available, or else they didn't know what to do with us. The waiting lounge that we found ourselves in was not well lit, so we weren't sure what to do.

Tajikistan was still in the middle of a civil war touched off by the collapse of the Tajik Soviet Socialist Republic in 1991. Like so many countries gaining independence from the former USSR, its infrastructure was almost nonexistent. Roads and transport were poor, medical and educational facilities were inadequate; even safe drinking water was unavailable to many. Although 93% of the landlocked country was covered by mountains, 90% of its people lived in the valleys. The average family scraped by on about seventeen dollars a month. Tajikistan had been considered the poorest republic in the Soviet Union; now that the union had collapsed the little country was cut off from help by the other republics they had formerly traded with, especially for wheat and natural gas used for heating homes and cooking. Inter-republic travel via train, plane and bus had also decreased.

After discussing the situation with Mike, Dave decided to take the children and me with him into the city to locate the house he had rented some months ago, on a scouting trip to this region. We left Mike at the airport to safeguard the luggage.

When the taxi arrived at our destination, it was not what I had envisioned. In fact, relatives of the landlord were living in the house along with their cows, chickens and other animals. They were probably taking refuge from skirmishes outside the city. At the same time, they must have reasoned, they could keep an eye on the house and prevent it from being ransacked by different factions.

When I realized that these people expected to live with us for the time being, I put my foot down.

"You need to get a different house," I told Dave. "We can't settle here with all these people and animals. We can't even speak their language! How can we keep the children healthy and control what they eat and drink?"

"Only one woman can be in charge of a kitchen" was a saying that came to mind. I needed to run my own household with my own kitchen rules if our family was to have any chance of surviving in this new land.

But it seemed we had little choice for the moment. Dave left Justin and me with the strangers to get some rest in one of the bedrooms. He took Rachel and went off to find an expat friend he knew who had rented a place in a different part of the city. However, Dave had no idea where that was. Jeff Paulsen was working at the American embassy as a paramedic, serving anyone who needed medical assistance. He and his family were also starting up an agency to help orphans in the country. He and Dave had been together during the scouting trip meant to set up future accommodations for their families. Jeff had then stayed on to fix up a place for his family, while Dave returned to the States so that he could travel with me and the kids to Tajikistan.

As Dave and Rachel rode around in a taxi up the main drag of the city, called Rudaki Street, they prayed that they would be able to find Jeff's place of residence. His family had arrived just a few weeks before we did. Dave had the taxi drive down several streets in the area trying to find Jeff and Conny's house. He was getting worried, because nothing looked familiar. Then all of a sudden he saw Jeff himself walking along one of the streets!

Years later, we found out that Jeff had stepped onto the street from his walled-in house quite by chance. He wanted to take a picture of the massive garbage heap just forty yards from his dwelling. Fortunately, in the middle of January, it didn't smell too bad. But just at the moment when Jeff was returning to his house, Dave spotted him from the taxi cab. Dave was overjoyed by this direct answer to prayer.

I am always amazed at how God leads us to do things as simple as taking photos; even, in this case, a photo of a mounting pile of garbage! He certainly guides us in mysterious ways.

Dave didn't waste words. "Do you know of any houses for rent?" he asked Jeff urgently. "I need one today!"

Jeff nodded. "Yes, I do. Just last night a lady came to my house and said that she would like to rent her house. In fact, it is the one that we are standing next to right now!"

Dave and Jeff went to the door, knocked, and asked if the house was still for rent. The lady said that it was, and rented it to our family on the spot for eighty dollars per month.

Later that same day Dave and Mike transported all of the luggage to our new house on Lutfti Street in the northern Wadanasos district of Dushanbe. The Paulsens invited us to supper at their home, just around the corner. They also introduced us to a Canadian family who was working for another mission.

Mike, Dave, Rachel, Justin and I soon began settling into our new home. The landlord and her children remained with us during the first days, until they could move. Before long, however, we noticed certain items were going missing. The lady's young son was enthralled with all of the "stuff" we had, that he didn't, and helped himself to several items. We didn't notice this right away due to the disruption of adjusting to new surroundings.-- Everything was so different from what we knew as "normal" in the United States. We had been thrust into a war zone where even basic foods like milk and eggs and common household items were hard to obtain in the open markets or bazaars.

Later, we spotted our video cassette for sale; the boy must have sold it to a vender. We felt like sitting ducks, so very vulnerable in those unfamiliar surroundings. Although we had studied the Dari language of the Afghans while in Peshawar, Pakistan, we still had a great difficulty understanding the Tajik dialect of Persian.

Russian was also commonly used as a trade language. So at first we were often misunderstood when we talked to people. We also misunderstood what people were saying to us. We realized it would take some hard work to learn the new Persian dialect. Thankfully the Lord equips His people when He calls them, and He provided us with excellent tutors.

The landlord's wife from our first house, in fact, became my tutor in Tajik. I loved it when she came around to help me with the language, because I was lonely. I missed just talking with people, especially before more international friends moved to Tajikistan. I am sure my kids felt the same way, although they didn't know how to put it into words. I was grateful that Rachel and Justin had each other to play with until they got to know more children.

CHAPTER 7

Candles in the Dark

Even now I feel overwhelmed as I recall those early years in Tajikistan. I have so many memories of how God sustained us, especially as we adapted to difficult living situations. Not only was the country at war, it suffered from floods, droughts, famine, earthquakes, epidemics, bombings and kidnappings. We learned to survive on very little, even with small children to care for.

When we left the States I hadn't fully realized the pain that six-year-old Rachel went through, saying goodbye to so many close relatives and little friends. Our son, Justin was two and a half years old and full of life. I was thankful that he and his sister were good playmates.

I tried to focus on ensuring that we had a healthy kitchen so that the children would not get sick from the unhygienic conditions around us. The vegetables and fruit we bought in the market had to be soaked in diluted iodine to kill germs, and we learned that the city's sewage pipes leaked into the pipes that provided our drinking water. It was necessary to boil it for twenty minutes to kill bacteria and then let the water cool until the mud settled in the bottom of the pot. Finally we poured the clear, cooled water into a water filter. This was the only way to avoid getting sick from the river water, which was all that came through the pipes in our part of the city.

After the first rains started in Dushanbe we saw mud-colored water trickling through our faucets and toilets. The river water resembled coffee, with a little milk in it.

I filled the bathtub with water and realized that the more I ran it, the darker the water looked. I wondered how in the world we were going to feel clean after bathing in this. We continued to go through the motions, but I think it was more a psychological exercise than anything else. We liked to think that we were somewhat cleaner after our muddy baths. After all, we reasoned, people in the West often paid to take mud spa baths, didn't they? Tajikistan gave it to us free, right from our taps! Eventually we followed advice to put in a tank for storing clean, clear rainwater for showers and baths. So we managed.

I told our children that under no circumstances when they took their baths were they to put water in their mouths, pretending to be whales or water fountains, because they could get very sick. Looking back now, I don't think bathing them in that dirty water was such a good idea but thankfully they stayed healthy, by the grace of God.

The house that we rented had an outdoor, enclosed toilet. Another small room held a bathtub and sauna that was heated when our gas supply worked.

Our neighbors watched our comings and goings from the upper floor of an apartment complex across from us. Every move we made, whether going for a bath, visiting the toilet or using the washing machine in our yard, was exposed to curious eyes. There was little doubt our lives were observed in a very public way during our many years in Dushanbe. Even our children were studied as they played in the part-cement, part-mud yard that was walled in and planted with some fruit trees. We were the entertainment of the day! Our neighbors called us the *"Americanskis,"* Russian for "Americans."

Raising a family in the midst of a civil war wasn't easy. Emotions ran high and it was an effort to remain calm, but we leaned on God's grace as much as we could. Reading His Word was essential. So was maintaining consistent personal and group prayer times.

Soon after we moved to Dushanbe we started a Sunday church meeting at our house because there was no English-speaking international church at this time. We wanted to maintain a regular worship time with other international believers in the country, most of whom were aid workers.

Our compound was designed perfectly for meetings because the main house had space for three bedrooms and a heated outdoor toilet with running water. This was quite a luxury! A guest house across the cement yard from our quarters was where we held some of those first church gatherings. The children used our home for Sunday School classes after the group singing time was over. I taught these sessions until other people volunteered. We had a rotating schedule for teaching the children, leading the worship part of the service and preaching.

Dave also maintained and developed good relationships with government officials who helped us obtain and keep visas. Work visas allowed us to live in the country so we could distribute vital aid like warm clothes and food. At the same time we continued to befriend all the Tajiks we met, whether they made a living as farmers, teachers, translators, sellers in the bazaars and shops, restaurant owners and many other occupations. In the villages their homes and animal shelters might be made of mud, with tin roofing. In the city one more often found apartment complexes, but the more wealthy owned their own walled-in homes with small yards containing vegetable and flower beds and fruit trees.

Whenever I entered a friend's home I was always expected to take my shoes off at the threshold; then I put them on again as I left. Although some homes used regular furniture, many others had carpeting with small cushion mats spread out on the floor for people to sit on. I would then be expected to help myself to tea and goodies on a tablecloth spread in front of the cushions. These cushions became beds for the family at night, spread with thick blankets for warmth in the winter time. During visits with our friends we were served all kinds of dishes like soup, yogurt, some sort of rice dish or kebabs with bread. Apples, oranges, lemons, grapes or pomegranates were normally served in a big fruit plate set in the middle of the tablecloth on the floor. Smaller dishes held almonds, raisins, boiled and dried chickpeas, walnuts, dried apricots and other snacks. One of my favorite dishes was called *osh*, which was rice with beef pieces that had been cooked together with cottonseed oil, rice, chickpeas, carrots and sometimes garlic bulbs, seasoned with spices like cumin, pepper and salt. Often this dish was served with a drained yogurt called *chaka*. *Naan* bread came with every meal and did it taste good! This was a round bread normally baked in a clay oven.

Dr. Asimov was a political dignitary whom we had met in New York City prior to coming to Tajikistan. His family befriended us when we first arrived in their war-devastated land. His wife persuaded their daughter to get fresh milk for us from the Russian hospital, where she worked as a doctor. Their son delivered it during the first few weeks we were in the country, so our children could have fresh milk instead of the powdered variety we had brought in our luggage. I was deeply moved by the kindness and generosity of this Muslim family. God used them to care for us in a very real way.

Many people in Tajikistan weren't being paid because of the country's collapsed economy. Our friend Jeff had a hired man who was friends with another person desperately looking for a job. So we were introduced to Latif, an English school teacher who became a faithful friend, translator, driver and mechanic for our Russian-made car.

Latif showed us how to shop for food in Dushanbe. His dear wife, Salamat, sent us jars of pickled vegetables she had canned, such as tomatoes, cucumbers, onions and garlic. Latif was a very gentle-spirited man, and loyal in friendship. In those early weeks of living in an embattled Dushanbe, he drove Dave around the city to find eggs, big burlap bags of flour, sacks of potatoes, rice and sugar, pounds of butter, vegetable oil and several liters of raw cottonseed oil so that we could have what we needed for cooking.

The city's electricity supply was far from consistent. I remember once when the power went off, the water also went off for several days. I was thankful at the time that we still had gas to cook and heat our homes.

"I hope the gas will never go off like the electric and water," I remember saying. Well, the gas, too, repeatedly vanished throughout the years we resided in Tajikistan!

During our first year a huge heavy rain fell in the mountains just north of Dushanbe, the Warzob River flooded so badly that it took out bridges, roads and part of the canal which brought water to our area of town. The municipalities had to shut our water off for around nine days, so we had to travel to other sections of town to obtain water for our house. We also had to take our clothes to another part of the city and wash them in someone else's apartment. With young children we had quite a bit of clothes-washing to do and could not put it off indefinitely. We were relieved when the water came back on after nine days, for it could have been longer. God sustained us, as always. We learned to appreciate any help we could get when there was no water to be had—from Tajiks, Russians or the few foreigners in the country at that time.

Tajikistan lacked many of the things we took for granted in the West. Even basic medicines and medical equipment were in short supply. Hospitals sometimes had to turn patients away or shut down for weeks at a time during epidemics. Meningitis, tuberculosis, typhoid, dysentery and respiratory illnesses were common killers.

While my family and I were spared these deadly diseases during our years in the country, like most workers we battled occasional stomach bugs. This came with the territory. But unfortunately I was also visited by more serious problems at various times. These included dysentery, urinary tract infections, skin allergies, bronchitis and hepatitis, gall stones, pneumonia and even food poisoning. Without ready access to the right medications these ailments could—and often did—drag me down.

"I don't see myself cut out for this work in Tajikistan!"
I once wrote in the journal I kept an escape valve.
"Lord, to get better here is almost impossible unless
you intervene for me. Please help me to sleep the whole
night through!"

Our friend Latif thoughtfully gave us a little puppy named Linda in the early days; sadly, she didn't survive very long because she got distemper. By then we had already bought a female German Shepherd from some Uzbeks in the bazaar. We liked animals. Some other friends had given us kittens, and we had bought some canaries from the bazaar. It felt like we had a mini zoo at our place. Little tortoises roamed the cement/mud yard. We even tried to raise chickens and goats but didn't do so well in keeping them alive. I had grown up with cows, horses, cats and dogs, but didn't know much about raising chickens and goats. So once they passed on, we decided to just stick with dogs and cats.

I remember one day walking by the canary bird cage on the table and noticing some blood and feathers on the cages' small metal wall. It became clear that a cat had eaten the bird for lunch on our carpet. I was so angry at him for pulling the little bird through the narrow wires of the cage. We let the other canary go free so that it could migrate to another place or try to find another partner. We didn't get any more canaries.

Our parakeets didn't fare much better. These birds didn't have the right water supplier for their rounded beaks, so they thirsted to death. As for fish, the tank became such a hassle to clean we also stopped the fun venture of raising them. Cats and dogs were enough for us.--Except that our German Shepherd Naida didn't really like cats. But Naida loved our family and was very loyal, protecting us faithfully from would-be thieves.

Eventually, we settled on the addition of one male dog to companion Naida, named Jack. Jack was another trusty German Shepherd and we had the two dogs for a long time, enjoying the many puppy litters they gave us. We sold and gave away many of their offspring over the years.

During our first spring, Rand and Rochelle Olson and their children came to Dushanbe to visit us from Samarkand, Uzbekistan. They were on a scouting trip to see if they could find accommodations in the same neighborhood as us. Another couple, the Neterers from the Midwest, also stayed in our home.

One evening the college-age Tajik girl who was cleaning and cooking for us decided to make a soup from a grass called "*sya alaf*," meaning "black grass." What I didn't know is that this was a natural laxative that the Tajiks love to eat in the spring to clean out their systems.

Well, this young girl, Narghese, questioned me as to how much *sya alaf* she should put into the soup. I told her to put a lot of it in, because it was so tasty. Well, throughout that night our guests beat a steady path to the bathroom. The next morning they had questions about the food we had served them for supper the night before.

The natural laxative grass soup worked quite well on our guests. Needless to say they were very "cleaned out," though a bit tired from a night of running to the toilet. Whenever we see each other today and this topic comes up, we always have a good laugh!

The Olsons and Neterers left for Samarkand to gather their possessions for the move to Dushanbe. We asked them to bring a good washing machine for us, because we couldn't find suitable appliances. The war was hindering international trade. They agreed to do this for us, and came back with the washer via train from Uzbekistan. It became a massive time-saver!

When the Olsons arrived they rented the house right next to ours. Mike had been living there by himself to keep it occupied until the Olsons came. Then he moved into a place behind theirs. All these houses' yards were connected at the corners of the property. Since there was a war going on, we foreigners decided it would be wise to live close together in one neighborhood.

Before Mike occupied this newly rented house that the Olson's said they wanted to rent, it was occupied by a group of single college students. Sadly, one of them had committed suicide in the bathtub. We helped the boy's family with funds to get his body back to their home in northern Tajikistan, so they could give him a proper funeral and burial. It was a tragic time, made all the more tragic because we had seen the despair felt by so many young people in this land. We prayed over this dwelling before Mike moved into it.

The students helped us plant a garden in our yard, but with the two dogs we owned, this didn't really take. Dave and I were still learning how to live in Central Asia as well as learning the Tajik language. At the same time we were busy establishing our humanitarian and development office. I was also struggling to keep up with Rachel's homeschooling curriculum. So we made a lot of mistakes.

Then Britt, a young woman from Sweden, joined us as a new teammate. She was a huge blessing, helping me with the children by keeping them company as I made sure we had food on the table for the team. Looking back now, even though I was Rachel's first grade homeschool teacher, I don't think I was the best influence on her. Homeschooling responsibilities added a lot of extra pressure to my schedule, which probably strained our mother-daughter relationship.

When the Olsons arrived with the Neterers from Samarkand, it felt great to have them living next door. Mike moved to a house just behind the Olson's. Our kids didn't feel so isolated when they had English-speaking playmates, who thought much the same way they did.

The Olsons had worked in Peshawar, Pakistan, like we had, so Lydia and Rachel already knew each other. Justin, Luke and Aaron had played together a few times in the States before we came to Tajikistan to open the work. The children spent a lot of time in each others' company while Rand and Rochelle set up their household and found work.

Mike and I continued helping Dave organize the Central Asian Development Agency. In the early months of '93 in Tajikistan CADA's official office was in Dr. Asimov's building, with our home serving as the main activity base. Rochelle and I shared responsibilities for extra-curricular school activities during the first years of home schooling. Ours was a busy household.

Before the Olson's family arrived, a boy that belonged to a family in one of the apartments across from our walled-in yard began to come over to play. He couldn't speak Tajik, but did speak Russian. When I visited his family's apartment and saw the décor it was apparent that his mother was involved in some type of witchcraft. She was a nice lady, but very much into the occult. Like much of Central Asia, Tajikistan was heavily influenced by Islam and sometimes local superstitions crept in. Only about 3% of the population Christians--mainly Russian Orthodox.

One night the electricity went out in our neighborhood, and this lady very kindly came to our rescue. We had not bought any candles at that point and were not prepared. The woman offered us a most interesting type of candle, made out of cotton pieces strewn over a plate covered with oil. Being a recipient of this act of kindness, I tried to become a friendly neighbor. I also shared some Christian literature so that she could see that there was a different way to live, dominated by peace and not fear.

Even today I have never forgotten that single thoughtful act when someone brought a homemade candle to lighten our darkness. How much more should believers in Christ reach out to others by sharing His light and love, in practical ways! Jesus himself said even a cup of water given in His name wouldn't go unnoticed by our heavenly Father. Small acts of kindness are seldom forgotten.

Rachel and Justin played with this lady's son off and on. He wanted to learn English, so with our children he was able to pick up a few words. As time went on, other Tajik and Uzbek children began to come around to play. Once the Olson family moved next to us there was a good same-culture group around the same age.

Having neighbors with a similar culture helped with some of the cross-cultural shock we were all adjusting to. As the international community continued to grow it became essential to find a bigger facility for Sunday worship meetings. Rochelle and Rand found a house for rent with ample room for holding services, as well as extra rooms for Sunday School classes. This facility was also used for the cooperative school that we helped start, along with other foreigners.

As more expatriate workers came to the country with different aid organizations, we were glad to help several families get settled into life in Dushanbe. The Great Commission was too big for anyone to accomplish alone and too important not to try to do together.

Before our first Thanksgiving in 1993, I tried to call home to touch base with my dear parents in Wisconsin. Unfortunately I wasn't able to get through. I thought probably my mom and dad had gone out to a bar or café for the evening. It was a great disappointment. Telephones only worked ten to twenty-five percent of the time and of course we didn't have cell phones or the internet to make Skype or FaceTime calls. Today workers in even very isolated places are blessed with more options for communication.

On Thanksgiving Day, Dave and I woke up to loud pounding on our compound door.

"Please, can you help me?" said a man standing outside, obviously desperate. "My wife—she's pregnant. She seems to have gone into premature labor!"

He motioned down the street where he and his wife had been waiting at a bus stop. Could he use our phone to call an ambulance?

After making the call he borrowed scissors and thread and ran back to the lady in distress. Soon afterwards he came rushing back with an infant wrapped in his winter leather coat! An old Russian woman—evidently a bystander—followed, leading the new mother who was still bleeding.

I took the woman inside our house and got her to lie down until the ambulance arrived. A lady doctor then delivered the placenta in our living room, and mother and baby were taken to the hospital.

What a way to start the day!

We hosted a special Thanksgiving dinner that afternoon, with some of the American Embassy staff as guests. Jeff came over to join us, too, although his family remained home. We stuffed ourselves with great food and had fun just hanging out and enjoying each others' company. Among our guests was Ambassador Stan Escudero and some of his top aids. At that time the American embassy staff lived on one of the floors of a big hotel, while the Russian embassy had a different floor in the same hotel. Both staffs worked and lived there as two rival country embassies. Quite an unusual arrangement, and I am sure it wasn't so hard for the two countries to spy on each other!

A few days later I got a phone call from my mother-in-law, Anne Lovett, in New Jersey. I was so happy to hear her voice, until she gave me some distressing news: my dad had suffered a heart attack. Anne gave me the phone number so I could call him at the hospital in LaCrosse, Wisconsin.

I was still trying to come to terms with this bombshell when Anne proceeded to tell me that my parents' house had caught on fire shortly before this event. The flames apparently started in the basement from a faulty lamp cord, right next to the office that supported their farm and gas station/mechanic business. Although nobody was injured Mom and Dad were no longer able to live in the place. It was probably the fire that precipitated my dad's heart attack.

As if this wasn't enough, I learned that the ambulance transporting my father to the hospital had gotten into an accident. Although Dad's life was once again spared, he would have to undergo four-way bypass surgery.

That same week my Uncle Christen Davig died. So many tragedies, all at once! It was during times like these that I felt torn in two, longing to be with my family thousands of miles away yet knowing I couldn't leave my responsibilities on the frontier. But I knew I could pray. God was able to be with my folks in Wisconsin just as He was with me on the other side of the world, in Central Asia. He was all powerful, and all knowing.

I tried to make a phone call to my father in the hospital, anxious to talk and pray with him. I wasn't able to get through for four hours because I had to book the calls through operators from Dushanbe to Moscow, and then to America. Finally, I told the operators that my father had suffered a heart attack and I was trying to contact him. Mercifully, they cooperated in connecting me to his hospital room phone. What a relief to talk and pray with him before his surgery!

Much later when he recovered from the procedure he said that he felt so much better. Fortunately, my parents had house insurance that helped to keep them afloat while Dad was out of work.

For months they stayed with my sister, then in a hotel and finally a camping trailer next to their farm house in Soldiers Grove, while they cleaned it and repaired the damage. When we returned to the States the following summer we were able to help them finish moving back in.

As our first Christmas in Dushanbe approached we decided we really wanted to hold a party for our new Tajik friends and the aid workers we had befriended. The kids in the expatriate community performed a play called "*Babushka*" (the Russian name for an old woman or grandmother), that focused on the nativity story of Jesus Christ. I played the guitar as the children sang, and Jeff's wife Conny directed the acting parts.

The play was performed in Rand and Rochelle's living room and everyone had a fabulous time, including both our Tajik and foreign friends. Of course, we supplied plenty of sweets and savory food to our guests as well, along with tea, cold drinks, and lots of laughter. It was a special celebration of Christmas and we felt as if we were truly becoming like a family.

If I remember right, our first Christmas tree in Dushanbe was potted, like the one we purchased in Peshawar. We hoped to plant this tree in our garden so that we could re-use it the next year, but it died. I was surprised that many Tajiks had imitation Christmas trees decorated with colorful lights. They didn't call it a Christmas tree, however; to them it was a New Year's tree. Under the control of Russia they had not observed the birth of Jesus, but everyone was allowed to celebrate the New Year as we did in the West.

I was so amazed to see the decorations, since Christmas time is one of my most favorite times of the year. It even snowed in Tajikistan before the holidays. When the snow fell on the streets it was so beautiful, light, soft, fluffy and clean to play in. But of course when it melted the landscape reverted to dirt and mud and giant potholes.

During the winters we took Jack, the male dog, out with us to play in the snow. There was a park near the house that we could walk to, and we let the kids use the big animal as their sled dog. He loved it. The hills weren't very long but we enjoyed sliding on them after the fallen snow left the air so fresh and clean.

Co-worker Britt taught us how to make snow lanterns from stacked snowballs. We learned to place a burning candle on the inside of a rounded, cone-shaped snowball "castle." Even to this day our family likes to make snow lanterns. We learned to make the most of small pleasures and created fun activities whenever we could.

On the first day of January 1994, of course, we celebrated Rachel's 7th birthday even though we were all tired from staying up to welcome in the New Year. We thought it was only fair to make much of our daughter--not wanting her to feel cheated by having a birthday so close to Christmas.

Our second spring of 1994 brought its own festivities with the celebration of *Navroz*. This celebration dates back to the Persian New Year, before Christ's birth. Many people in Tajikistan took this opportunity to welcome the fresh spring weather after the long winter. Many times people made a special dish from new wheat shoots that they boiled all night. They ate this with their rice dishes and dipped pieces of *naan* into it. It tasted great. Many people also displayed small clay pots with green wheat shoots in their houses. Navroz parties commonly took place with dancing and the reciting of poems. We enjoyed this celebration with our new friends.

The early 1990's remained very volatile and hostile both inside and outside the city, requiring us to keep curfew hours. We didn't leave our house from after dark until 5:00 the next morning.

Whenever I think of the first four years I acted as Rachel's homeschool teacher, I become sad. I had no idea that she was dyslexic and could not understand why she was having so much difficulty with reading and writing. I was very focused on helping my family survive in a safe and healthy way during those war days, when resources and healthy food were scarce. As a result, I was impatient when she wrote and read letters backwards. Needless to say, Rachel, too, grew very frustrated.

Later on, a teacher named Sally from New Zealand helped us realize that Rachel was probably dyslexic. She took over the teaching of Rachel and Justin along with the other expatriate children--a very big blessing for all of us! I could then focus on just being Rachel's mom, and help her with homework and make sure we had all we needed in our safe haven called home. But the emotional damage had already been done. To this day it brings tears to my eyes to remember my lack of patience when my little girl struggled so hard.

My advice to parents who have a child who may be dyslexic or suffering from ADHD is to stop jumping all over them. Some of us are simply not cut out to be homeschooling moms. Yet this is a common arrangement in frontier situations where good local schools are not an option.

I am thankful for teachers like Sally, who came to Dushanbe when our kids needed a professional teacher for their grade school years. I only supervised internet schooling for Justin, so he didn't have to endure my impatient teaching style.

Although I believed in Rachel's abilities I didn't encourage certain parts of her education because I didn't have the skills. By Gods' grace, however, Rachel has not only survived but thrived. Today she is a preschool teacher herself as well as teaching in a daycare before and after school program. She enjoys her good paying job in Wisconsin and earned a Masters degree at Carroll College in Waukesha, in the fall of 2021.

As mentioned before, Rachel and Justin made friends with Tajik and Russian neighbors as well as hanging out with expatriate children. This was good for them. In fact, we all benefitted from rubbing shoulders with friends from other cultures and languages. We parents in the cooperative homeschool community agreed that we wanted our kids to try to learn some Tajik and Russian language skills so that they could integrate with neighboring children and coworkers' friends. This made it possible for them to go to the bazaar, ride public transport, play games with local children on the street and make purchases at local grocery stores. They were learning a lot about the society they were living in, even though they were not Tajiks by birth.

I can appreciate what our offspring were probably going through. An international move to a strange land where most people didn't speak English, and who dressed and acted very differently from people in the West, was quite an adjustment. Even for myself.

The ladies in this part of the world wore loose, very colorful dresses over loose-fitting slacks, and a small scarf on their heads. I wore this traditional dress at parties that we went to, especially in the villages. It felt good to identify with the ladies in their homes. In the city I normally wore western clothes, because most of the educated Tajiks chose that style of dress. I tried to use my broken Tajik language with the ladies, and they were quite patient with me when I made mistakes in pronunciation.

I was always impressed with the quantities of snacks and main dishes we were offered when we were guests in their homes. When Tajiks served tea they poured it from porcelain teapots into a cup three times, then returned it to the teapot before they gave you the cup of tea, especially if your cup was the first. After a meal was finished the people said an "amen" by raising their hands and giving a downward motion close to their faces, showing their thankfulness for the food they had received. I liked this tradition of remembering God in their lives.

In addition to hosting the international church during those early years, we were involved in small Bible studies with believers that spoke Tajik and Russian. I loved meeting with local ladies. I remember when I was beginning to teach the Sunday School class, the lesson was on accepting how God has made us rather than wanting to be different. It was important to understand that He made us the way He did for a special purpose.

I shared about Amy Carmichael, an Irish missionary to India years before. When she was little she prayed that God would change her brown eyes to blue, like her brother's. She was disappointed when her prayers weren't answered. But God knew that one day she would be used to rescue Indian children from temple prostitution and slavery. He gave her brown eyes so that she would fit in better.

With this in mind, I guessed that God purposely made me with an adventurous and persevering personality. That's what saved me during those traumatic days in Tajikistan. The Mafia flourished. Bombs went off and people were killed in drive-by shootings. Once I wrote in my journal, *"Lord, I can't believe you have placed us in a war zone. Please keep us safe in the hollow of your hands."*

Girls and women on the streets were sometimes molested or dragged into cars and raped. Dirty water was a constant health hazard. Basic supplies continued to be hard to find in the bazaars.

At the same time, more and more aid workers kept arriving in the country, so we didn't feel quite so alone.

Sometimes when another foreign family discovered cheese or bananas or some other special treat in the bazaars, they let us know. We made our way there as quickly as we could to purchase what we could. I remember when a single banana sold for 75 cents or even a dollar. Needless to say, we didn't buy many bananas! But when items like cheese from Holland was occasionally flown in, we often seized the opportunity to stock up.

I remember that Rachel and Justin loved the little chocolate eggs with toy prizes hidden inside. Dave sometimes found these treats at the airport bazaar or at the Dushanbe International Hotel, which was actually a very dull and dingy looking building in its early days.

During our first year we drove to the mountains to go hiking. Tajikistan's mountains were steep and beautiful in all seasons and we liked to explore. I missed being able to ride a horse, but this was not a culturally acceptable activity for women. Later we bought a small *dacha*, a summer cement shelter, as a getaway, especially during the typhoid epidemic. This place had a springfed pond where it was safe to go swimming. This helped us cool off in the summertime.

On our outings our family liked to stop at kebab cafés for refreshments even though there were always soldiers at checkpoints. The army kept watch over entrances to the city to protect it from the opposition's attacks against the government.

One time while hosting two men from an American aid organization, we decided to take them as tourists to the mountains in the Warzob River valley, north of Dushanbe. Along the way we stopped for food at a café by the riverside. The political situation was still sensitive, and as we sat at an outside table an armored personnel carrier pulled up with several soldiers inside. The men jumped off and walked into the café. Soon they were questioning customers and the atmosphere started heating up. The soldiers began pushing around a man who had been sitting at one of the tables.

Watching this interaction with our two children and two guests, we were afraid of what might happen next. A fearful tension hung in the air. We started to pray for God's protection for ourselves and the people around us.

Suddenly the man who was being threatened by the soldiers came over to our table. In a low voice, he begged us to tell the soldiers that he was our driver. Meanwhile those same soldiers were walking towards us with a threatening glare. Dave put the stranger off and we continued to pray for safety.

As the minutes passed without further aggression, customers began to settle down again. We decided to get up and take our kids and our guests back to Dushanbe. We didn't want to take further chances after such a scary incident. We never learned what happened to the man after we left, but once again, God had protected His own in a sticky situation.

After a few more days, our visitors left the country and we went back to distributing food and clothing to victims of the conflict. By this time we had successfully gotten through all the red tape and were officially registered with the government as the Central Asia Development Agency.

Besides doing aid work, Dave wanted CADA to facilitate business opportunities in order to rebuild the country's economy. In September of 1993 we hosted a delegation of business people from the United States, in order to explore the possibilities of more business ventures starting up at an international level. Although this would benefit local manufacturers it didn't really work out. Local Tajik businessmen didn't understand how to transact international business because they had been so cut off from modern business practices during seventy years of Communist rule. International affairs were a new ballgame.

The Western businessmen presented seminars concerning integral business operations. After their time in Dushanbe, a chartered plane flew our guests and our family to the northern part of the country, over the mountains, to tour the country's second largest industrial city, Khujand. Khujand was one of the oldest cities in Central Asia and was known for being the home of scientists, writers and musicians. Besides being the scientific and cultural center of Tajikistan the region was known for lush orchards of apricot trees. I tasted this fruit and agreed they were the sweetest apricots that I had ever eaten. The place looked very different from Dushanbe because the mountainous terrain was further away from the city limits.

After visiting potential Tajik business partners in the city, it was time to return to Dushanbe with our American visitors and Tajik government dignitaries.

Our friend Rand Olson had come with us on the flight to Khujand, but then went on to Uzbekistan in order to collect cargo at the Tashkent airport. The cargo had arrived from Peshawar, Pakistan, for both his family and ours.

Before he ventured across the Tajik border to pick up these items, Rand and Dave agreed that the chartered plane with the delegation would wait for his return from Tashkent. They could then fly the many boxes of personal items from Khujand to Dushanbe.

Rand must have run into a problem with all these possessions, however, when he crossed the border back into Tajikistan. The chartered plane loaded with the delegation waited as long as it could on the tarmac, while Dave tried to persuade the pilots to delay taking off from Khujand. The pilots insisted that they needed to return to Dushanbe and couldn't wait any longer for Rand.

Eventually the pilots started the engines and the plane started to taxi down the runway, preparing for takeoff. As the plane moved, we suddenly caught sight of Rand running after us like an 007 agent in a spy movie. We shouted to a Tajik friend to tell the pilots to stop the plane.--Our friend had arrived!

Believe it or not, the pilots did halt the aircraft. They opened the doors to the passenger area and allowed our precious cargo to be loaded on board. We were so relieved. What a miracle! God could pull us through even when the odds were stacked against us; He could even change the hearts of those who don't know Him. I needed to remember this lesson.

Later as we talked with Rand he told us he had run right through airport security and onto the tarmac without anyone trying to stop him. This wasn't too surprising since security wasn't very strict in those days. The locals probably thought that he was just another crazy foreigner. I smile to myself even now, remembering this example of God's grace.

By this time we were receiving new team members seconded from other organizations. We were pleased that CADA was gaining in credibility and consolidating into a small group of people with the same vision: to relieve suffering and improved the lives of the people of Central Asia, both physically and spiritually. Most newcomers made it a priority to learn the Tajik language and culture. A growing team was an encouragement to us, but it was not without challenges. Each person came with a different idea of how they wanted to work in our organization.

As the Central Asian Development Agency team grew, so did other non-government organizations. We enjoyed fellowship with families like the Paulsens, Jespersens and Olsons, even though they were with other agencies.

The increasing number of aid groups on the ground meant that more and more children were coming to Tajikistan with their parents. So our children had others to play with and the international cooperative school expanded. Each student eventually, got to use a curriculum in their own language.

The co-op school used volunteer teachers, but many of us parents also shared the responsibility of instructing different subjects. This allowed us to cover everything the children needed like English, arithmetic, reading, writing, Tajik and Russian languages and history. We made sure to include physical education to keep the students in shape, as well as art and music. I was on the cooperative school's committee.

As mentioned before, a woman from New Zealand eventually came to serve as a first full-time teacher. We moms were overjoyed, because none of us wanted to send our kids to boarding school.

Other new recruits for our CADA team in 1994 proved equally invaluable, for Mike McCleland, our first team member, had left at Christmas. We appreciated all that he and our new team members brought to the success of our efforts to help desperate victims of war. We needed increasing numbers of team workers to help carry the load of serving the Tajik people.

Our Tajik staff was now composed of Latif, Saeid Khoja and Shoista. Although they were the first local people to join the Central Asia Development Agency, these three were eventually joined by many others. Shoista had worked with the local government at one time and was our main translator; her brother worked in the country's ministry of television.

We were honored to make friends with many wonderful Tajiks through the years. I will never forget them and even today stay in contact with many via Facebook, Skype, email, letters and telephone calls. These men and women are still in my heart, though some have gone on to glory. We know it's not likely we will ever see most of the others again on this side of heaven.

One of them, whom we'll call Azad, was a young married man we happened to meet at a house gathering. We didn't see Azad for a long time after that first encounter, but when a women's-only event was scheduled we needed a good cook for the food that was going to be served over a few days. He agreed to cook for all of us.

From the preparation area outside our meeting place, Azad enjoyed listening to the worship songs we sang. He was amazed by the beautiful behavior he saw demonstrated by the women when they gathered in the courtyard for tea time and lunch. After those days he decided in his heart he wanted to have this same type of love. Today Azad this man is reaching other people with the hope of Christ.

At another women's celebration I met a young gal who had been in a relationship that wasn't healthy. By God's grace I was able to help her get free from that situation. Today she and her husband are both sharing God's good news to many people in their own country. God has kept His hands on them.

One friend I made was a Muslim by her cultural upbringing, but she was curious about what Christians believed. Over time, after reading God's Word and spending hours in heart-to-heart chats with me about life's issues, she decided to give her heart to Christ and live by His ways.

One day she came to our house after reading some materials on how to let your family know that you have become a Jesus-follower. She told us, "Yes! I am ready."

We had other friends at our house that day, so together we prayed with her. God met this dear woman's need to start a personal relationship with Him, and she trusted that He would help her take a stand with her family.

Whenever new team members joined or old members left there were always adjustments to be made. We called the three stages "Forming, Storming and Norming." Each step had important aspects in helping people adapt to one another in developing work relationships. In the "Forming" stage new recruits were just getting used to the rest of the team. The "Storming" stage was when individuals tried to understand each other's differences and view these differences as an asset to the team's life. The Norming stage is when members have actually worked out and accepted each other's strengths for the sake of building the team's effectiveness.

Following the urging of our government friend Dr. Assimov we had already distributed tons of clothing, shoes, blankets, and food items to Tajikistan's war victims, operating out of our own house for a while and then from a house downtown off Rudaki Street. The country's president actually moved into this popular neighborhood later on. But we soon realized that we needed to expand to a bigger space. Thanks to a deal Dave was able to make with the Tajik government, we were able to relocate our CADA office to one of their buildings. In this new building we were able to start an internet program, providing the first email node in the country. Services were offered free of charge to students, government people, businesses, teachers and professors.

Another project was the refurbishing of computers. Used equipment was sent from the West to help impoverished people in the country learn to use computers and connect with others in the republics and internationally. Many of the reconditioned computers were gifted to universities, schools, businesses and individuals eager to learn.

All of these developments enhanced our acceptance by the government. Officials were aware that our agency was doing essential work in building the country's infrastructure.

To help people in rural areas we started a small business venture for village women, hoping they could eventually sell their hand woven products to tourist shops. Once this project was underway we realized the need for quality control, so I went with two of our Tajik staff to help with this aspect. I was amazed by how many women were involved. Many of their husbands had abandoned them to go to Russia for work and never came back. By selling their handmade items, they were able to provide necessities for their families. We needed to impress these ladies with the importance of good quality so their gift items would sell. I can report that several of these women are even today continuing to sell their products to stores catering to people looking for gifts.

First aid tips were also taught in the villages to help people to survive health issues like burns and severe diarrhea. One time a young child suffered burns in the village and two of our nursing staff were able to introduce the treatment of cold water applications instead of oil and mashed potatoes. The village people saw the difference: The cold water method cooled the skin faster and more effectively restored the burned areas.

Relief work in action was helping people buy what they needed, whether it was flour, oil, hygiene kits, blankets, clothes or shoes. Development work was providing training in a skill. It was the difference between giving someone a fish or giving him a pole and teaching him to fish so he could sustain himself. Ladies who learned the importance of making good quality handwoven items or how to raise goats or harvest honey from bees were receiving tools that could help their families on a permanent basis.

Dave decided to offer English language classes as part of CADA's development program. Everyone in the country seemed keen on learning English because it was the international trade language. It would allow them to get better jobs.

Americans Craig and Joyce, Chuck Sauer and others were instrumental in getting the English training center off the ground. After some Tajiks went through the program we hired a few of them as English teachers, too. Sabo, who knew Russian, Tajik and English quite well, was one of our local instructors. I also taught at the English center when I had time away from the Cooperative Christian School.

Of course, as the number of Christ followers in Tajikistan grew, other needs became obvious. Tajik Gospels, children's Bibles and discipleship literature of all kinds was in short supply. We decided to publish our own materials and soon I was overseeing a team of Tajik translators and editors. I also duplicated hundreds of gospel videos into Tajik, Russian, Uzbek and English languages for distribution around the country. Rachel liked to help me with the duplication of videos.

For those who were willing, there was no end to the work that had yet to be tackled. I saw children begging on the streets and abused little girls who had no one to rescue them. I even felt sorry for black market dollar changers; I am sure that their lives weren't the best. And mafia people may have had money, but they lived in fear for their lives because of the bigger, even more corrupt bosses above them. I wanted to be available to everyone in need, but my time and energies were being spread too thin.

CHAPTER 8

Growing Pains

Breaks from the field made all the difference in helping the family cope with the cumulative stresses of life in Tajikistan. They also gave us a chance to see doctors and dentists and take care of other important business.

Our first trip back to the States in the summer of 1994 did not exactly go according to plan. Seven-year-old Rachel was sick on the flight to Moscow, and somehow, distracted by caring for her and Justin, I was unaware that the leather pouch holding our travel documents had slipped under the seat. Our passports, tickets for the onward flight to New York and money were all in this pouch.

Discovering our loss after landing in Moscow we reported it to the airline authorities. Our fervent prayer was that it would be found. Meanwhile we raced around the city to apply for new passports, and find a place to spend the night. We were just about to return to the airport to pay $800 in fines for new exit visas, when the impossible happened.

The pouch was turned into the airport information desk-- with all of its contents intact. After getting back our old passports with the right visa stamps, we returned to the American embassy to cancel the new ones we'd just applied for. What a day that was! Nine o'clock that night we were once again on our way. God continued to keep His protective hands on us.

Spending time with my parents on the farm that summer was precious. We rode horses, swam, canoed and fished to our hearts' content. Best of all we could help Mom and Dad finish moving back into their refurbished farmhouse.

We also enjoyed precious reunions with far-flung friends including Dave's side of the family in New Jersey. Although there was never enough time to do everything and see everyone we wanted to, we returned to Dushanbe feeling recharged and refreshed.

As time went on our CADA team members included Americans, Germans, Japanese, Chinese, Koreans, British, Malaysian, Swedish, Tajiks and Russians. This meant there was plenty of room for misunderstandings within this vast cultural and linguistic spectrum. Even though we worked together to make a positive contribution to our adopted land, divisive problems inevitably cropped up. It was sometimes hard to maintain a positive outlook. Yet it was essential to resist caving in to fear, anger and resentment towards co-workers--or towards God.

I remember one small example of this, from the point of view of a mother. My greatest hurdle each morning was getting our kids up, dressed, fed and ready for school. Some of our single team members who lived nearby, however, had a habit of showing up at the house during this early morning routine. Lounging in the doorway, they talked and waited for Dave to give them a ride to the office. It was clear they had no idea of how much they were in the way. If I didn't get the children out the door they would be late for school.

I didn't feel that these CADA workers needed to hitch a ride with Dave, since public transport was available as other people in Dushanbe used to get to work. I think they were just feeling very insecure about their safety in those days. But we finally decided to advise team members not to come to our home when we were getting our kids off to school.

Many workers didn't like this new rule, of course. But we felt it was necessary to separate our family life somewhat from the team, and not have them around us all the time. I still don't know if this was the right decision, but we did need some space, especially in the morning. We had to protect our time with our kids when they most needed us.

On another occasion I had to talk to Rachel and Justin about a person on our team that they didn't like. This man had recently taught their Sunday school lesson. When I asked them why they disliked him they couldn't really give me a reason.

We were to learn after some time that this individual was struggling with sexual abuse issues from the past, and the kids sensed something was wrong. I realized then I needed to listen to them. Even before this experience I had learned at a missionary family life seminar that when children don't trust someone, you should pay attention. They are often aware of "bad vibes" that parents don't always catch.

Eventually the person under discussion was asked to leave our field. It was apparent that he needed to go home to get professional help for past abuse issues. He did receive the counseling he needed, and was rehabilitated to the point where he could start over. He later wrote Dave in order to thank him for his intervention.

In the mid-90's we were disappointed when two of our CADA families decided to leave for "greener pastures" in another organization. At the same time I and another family fell ill with hepatitis A. Someone in the office plugged in a computer without the transformer, and it blew. Then to top it off, $1000 was stolen from our safe.

"Dave is ready to quit and so am I…." I wrote in my journal. *"But it's another opportunity to trust God for His purposes to be worked out."*

In spite of the Enemy's attacks and a larger team composed of different nationalities and personalities, each with his or her own opinion of how a team should be run, we did manage to keep some sort of unity. We soldiered on, knowing that whenever new members joined there would always be stages of "Forming, Storming and Norming" as we all got used to juggling new relationships.

While our CADA team continued to grow, a volunteer teacher with another organization helping at the co-op school suggested to Dave and I that our daughter Rachel might need to be tested for dyslexia. This was on our agenda when the family went back to the States for a short break in the summer of 1998.

The testing for Rachel confirmed that she was mildly dyslexic. We were glad to know what steps to take and the tools she was given from the Davis Dyslexia Correction program helped our daughter continue learning in leaps and bounds in all subjects. She already excelled at sports, developing relationships with people and learning the Tajik language.

By 1999 Dave was mainly supervising Central Asian Development Agency while a co-worker from Singapore ran the mission side of the work. He and his wife were pastorally responsible for the foreign volunteers joining us on the field. He arranged language and culture orientation tutors, found house helpers and in general provided the basic training newcomers needed to adjust and maneuver around Tajikistan. Up to that point, Dave and I were sharing those responsibilities. Thankfully, a Tajik language program for foreigners had also been started by another agency, which was very helpful.

Some of the pressure was also relieved when CADA was moved under the umbrella of another organization headquartered in Europe. This was a good fit. The change released Dave from overall administrative responsibilities so he could concentrate more on the development and facilitation of resources on the ground.

The humanitarian needs in Tajikistan continued to multiply in 2001, when serious fighting once again broke out between rival factions. Sometimes we could hear guns blasting away only ten miles from our house. In addition, the KGB and Muslim fundamentalists, alarmed by the growth of Christianity in the country, had begun harassing fellowships. One church was singled out for a bomb attack during a Sunday morning service: ten people were killed and a hundred wounded. A Christian relief agency was closed down, its workers ordered to leave the country.

Although CADA escaped this fate, it suffered other kinds of attacks. The wife of a team member was in a major road accident that destroyed their vehicle. The three year old child of another family had to be air-ambulanced out of the country when a pot of boiling water overturned on him. Fifty percent of the little boy's body sustained third degree burns. Tragically, five months later, he died.

Then, early one morning during the first week of September 2001, I was suddenly wakened by a terrifying dream. I told Dave I had seen our several aid workers standing on top of a very tall building. An airplane flew towards us, and as it circled a wing crashed into the building. The top floors were cut off and fell below, but the aid workers were unhurt.

Dave reassured me that there were no tall buildings in Tajikistan. We would have to go to New York City to find skyscrapers!

But a few days later we stared at our television screen in disbelieving shock. A plane had deliberately flown into the upper stories of New York's World Trade Center, setting it on fire. We watched numbly as one of the tallest buildings in the world slowly crumble into dust.

Most Tajiks condemned the terrorist attack. Soon afterwards, the country became a strategic base for the Northern Alliance's fight against extremist Islam. Meanwhile, thousands of desperate Afghans converged at the borders without food, clothing or shelter. CADA was one of the few relief agencies on the spot. We moved quickly to save lives, sending truckload after truckload of supplies across the hazardous terrain. Some Afghan families camped in freezing temperatures all through that winter.

When a major earthquake hit the north in the spring, Dave pleaded for emergency medical workers and supplies to supplement CADA's already over-stretched resources. Through this effort alone 500,000 men, women and children received the help they needed to go on living.

With each passing year on the field Dave and I improved our language and cultural skills; this made is possible to build deeper friendships with the Tajik people around us. Our kids were getting older so we had a bit more time to cultivate older relationships even as we made new ones. God continued to undertake for us, especially when problems popped up unexpectedly at home or at work.

I remember when a fire broke out on the rooftop of our house, just above Rachel's bedroom. None of us were home except two house helpers, and two women painting the outside walls of our house.

That day I was teaching English at our office downtown, when Saeid Khuja came into my classroom to alert me to the fact that a fire had broken out at our house. Instead of springing into action like a normal person, I just stood there staring with disbelief, stunned and emotionless. I continued automatically to teach my class as if nothing had happened. Then one of my female students, who was a doctor, said, "Pam, don't you think you should go home to deal with this emergency situation?"

After thinking about her question for a bit, I responded. "Yes, I think you are right."

Off I went, leaving my students, and rushed to our house in the northern part of Dushanbe. A fire truck was parked on the street outside.

Dave and Saeid were already there, assessing the situation. As I walked into the courtyard I saw that our tin roof had been partly ripped upwards. The outside electrical line was lying on the ground, and ladders were leaning against the side of the house to reach the lower part of the roof. Hoses had been spraying affected areas with water. Black rubble strewed the ground and a crowd of people milled around.

I thanked God that the kids were at school. Rajabgul, our cook, and Cveta, the cleaner, were beside themselves, clearly distraught by what had taken place. Two female painters were also there but since they only spoke Russian I couldn't understand what they were trying to say.

Rajabgul and Cveta proceeded in detail to describe their version of things, in Tajik. They said they had been inside attending to their individual jobs while the painters were working outside. Suddenly one of the women noticed an electrical fire on the roof, and knew there was imminent danger of the whole house going up in flames.

"You know that all morning the water had been off," the women told me. "But after one of the painters saw the fire she noticed your hose now had water flowing from it. She put a rubber glove on her hand and started to spray the spot where the fire was, hoping to keep it at bay. The flames were just above Rachel's room, coming from the outside wall of the house where the electric wires were."

Cveta tried to call a humanitarian agency office that was just around the corner from our house, but the phone wouldn't work. So she went out onto the street and told people that there was a fire starting on the wall of our house.

A Tajik man happened to be standing on the street. He had just gotten his cast off from a broken arm. He came into our courtyard, found our rubber-handled axe and proceeded to intervene in keeping the fire from spreading.

"He took that axe and began to chop through the wires until they became disconnected from the house," said the ladies. "Thank God that he was available to help!"

I did thank God. The stranger had known exactly what to do.

Miraculously, the water supply that had been off all morning returned just in time to slow the fire as it caught onto the rafters. The Lord had once more shown us His mercy and grace, protecting us as we were about His kingdom business. This further example of all He did for us strengthened our faith.

Although the fire in the rafters did cause the roof to leak when the rains came that spring, we were grateful to still have a house, with a roof over our heads.

We could also see that God was at work in other peoples' hearts during those difficult years. A young man who had had his leg badly shot up by soldiers was lying in a hospital, getting medical help. Some of our friends went to Rostam's bedside to talk and pray with him and he received Christ as his Lord. He began to attend church with his friends, so we had the privilege to meet him. He helped with editing some discipleship material. As the young person recuperated from his injury he continued to grow in his faith. But then he started to struggle in some areas of his life. The small church counseled him to move back to his home area in the north of Tajikistan. When he returned home he found another church group to be a part of.

God met Rostam in a mighty way as the local believers prayed for the complete healing of his leg. The leg was totally restored so that he could once again walk normally. Thrilled, he returned to Dushanbe to show the rest of us how God had healed him. We were amazed, of course, and rejoiced with him. Rostam found a job with an organization as a guard. He worked with integrity and we were so glad for him.

Later on we were shocked by the news that Rostam had been tragically killed on his job. The young man had been such a shining light of God's love and healing power! His death was a struggle to accept, but we realized that this situation didn't take God by surprise.

2001 continued to be a significant year. We were able to purchase a large old Russian bathhouse in the city of Dushanbe, in order to move our offices from the Tajik government building. God provided the money for this building in an amazing way.

We were attending an international conference in Malaysia, with our children. It was a break that we desperately needed as a family and we totally enjoyed the warm weather and resort facilities. Justin and Rachel swam in the welcoming sea, ate lots of delicious food, walked on the sandy beach and of course watched their fill of English-speaking TV which wasn't available on local stations in Tajikistan. They even got to ride a jet runner and tried para-sailing. Doing fun things was essential in keeping our kids healthy.

During the conference we "happened" to meet a businessman named Todd Hendricks, from Pennsylvania. This was a God thing, because our long conversations eventually spurred this young man to help finance the building we wanted to buy. In 2002 he and several friends made a trip to Tajikistan to see the various relief and development projects we were involved in. As a family, we even accompanied the men to northern Afghanistan.

The two outposts we visited were simple mud houses surrounded by mud walls, but the office and house compound was spacious. Our visitors were impressed by the fruit trees and vegetable garden planted by our staff. The house had no running water and water from the well in the yard was too salty to drink, so we had it brought from a nearby stream for tea.

But Todd and our other guests were most impacted by seeing a program CADA had initiated in the northern villages of Rustaq and ChaAb, called Food for Work. The elders of these villages didn't want to just receive free handouts for their families, they wanted to earn their bread. It was emotionally important for them to feel useful after suffering the losses of war. So, the men helped to reconstruct roads for vehicles and create water supplies for villages. Our expatriate staff helped with medical aid and taught hygiene classes that saved many lives. The CADA workers were Westerners and Tajik and even included a Japanese midwife. The team visited widely scattered villages, making friends while helping Afghan women learn how to safely deliver their babies and keep them healthy after birth. One of the Tajik doctors told me that she was totally shocked by how uninformed the people were in their ideas of hygiene, even though they lived a few hours from the Tajik/Afghan border. Many times when a child was born someone would cut the umbilical cord with a rusty axe or dirty knife. Little wonder that so many babies and mothers died from infections.

The Afghan men who drove vehicles for us didn't want our female staff to wear the all-encompassing *burkas* or cloaks over their clothes, when they rode in the CADA landcruiser. They explained that they wanted village people to know he had expatriates with him, not immoral Afghan women. A good Afghan woman would never be seen in the company of a strange man. In fact, they would not even ask for help from a male doctor. This very strict code of separation between men and women was not practiced in Tajikistan, which had been settled by Russians and Tajiks together. One Tajik man told us that Tajiks didn't want these ancient ways for their womenfolk. They wanted a more modern way of life.

It was a whole new world for our visitors from the West. Seeing both Afghanistan and Tajikistan for themselves opened their eyes forever. It was as though they had travelled back in time to a place without even the most basic conveniences. They travelled roads that were not really roads, carved out of the desert. They met people who struggled simply to survive from one day to the next. And they wanted to do something to help.

I am reminded of a quote made by missionary extraordinaire Hudson Taylor, years ago: "God's work done in God's way will never lack God's supply." Many times through the years I have felt like giving up. Dave and I knew that in ourselves we were totally inadequate to truly help the poor. But if it is God's work, He will provide. We could bank on it!

The building we purchased to house the CADA office, with Todd Hendrick's help, required extensive renovations; but it was big enough to allow for growth. Both foreign and local people from our team helped to supervise the work, and it would never have been rebuilt without their help. I particularly liked the location of the new building because it was closer to our house.

When the CADA office finally moved into the new facility in 2003, we were all overjoyed. The exterior was painted a startling bright pink instead of the burgundy Dave had planned, but in the end the color grew on us and the sun gradually faded it to a lighter shade.

English classes, a large internet hub, the relief and preventative health offices, Dave's personal station, computer and business training rooms and the main administration offices were all operating in full force by 2003. We even had our own cafeteria to ensure that employees and volunteers were fed healthy food while they worked with us, without having to go out to local restaurants all the time. Our main cook was Adolat, who has since passed on into eternity. She learned much about Jesus Christ while she worked for us, but I don't know what transpired in her heart. I heard that two of our foreign friends went to her bedside to pray with her, at the end. Adolat heard Jesus's invitation to all, "Come unto me all you who are heavy laden and I will give you rest." I trust that she responded.

By this time, our daughter Rachel had chosen to finish her last two years of high school at a boarding school in Germany called Black Forest Academy. She wanted to be around other international kids her age, and in her position of being a "third culture kid"--raised in a *culture* different from her nationality, and living in a different environment during much of her childhood. The Christian academy was well known for offering a high quality education to international children, but we all missed her so much living so far away from our home.

After graduation in 2005 Rachel returned to Tajikistan. At nineteen she began teaching conversational English classes at our office, to adults much older than she was. Feedback from students told us that she was considered one of the best English teachers they had experienced. She was a natural, and thrived on her interaction with people from so many walks of life.

Because we experienced one or two bomb threats at the old office, we decided to put in a security system at the entrance of our new building. Security was always a concern in Tajikistan's political climate, even though the tension was beginning to ease.

Then, in 2006, we were unexpectedly forced to leave the country. A major issue had evolved over land that one of our houses sat on, used to support humanitarian and ministry projects. Tajikistan's president had built a house near this property on Rudaki Street, and his daughter had wanted the land for some years. So we were booted out of the way by a KGB officer close to the president's family, who declared the house too near the president's residences and eminent domain. We had actually been in the process of selling this property to a banker and had even received the purchase price in our USA bank account. But everything came to a halt. We were required to wire all the money back because Tajik law offices stopped the sale from being legal. We chose to leave with integrity on our side. Later we learned that the KGB officer had admitted to orchestrating our departure.

It also became obvious that some people in the government disapproved of our active Christian witness. Our visas for living in the country were not renewed, and after staying four months longer without stamps we received an ultimatum from authorities, giving us only a few more days. Thankfully, a few days turned into two weeks to prepare for the move. During the final frantic days of packing up we attended many going-away parties thrown by friends we loved.

Many tears were shed by all of us, and I still get emotional remembering those last days. I wanted so much to stay on and continue the friendships we had developed over our thirteen years in Tajikistan. We had seen many positive changes as the country moved from the horrors of civil war. A ceasefire was reached back in 1997, and peaceful elections were held in 1999. But the fighting had taken an estimated 100,000 lives. Some 1.2 million other men, women and children were refugees both inside and outside the borders.

We were grateful that we were able to see some of the people in this land come to Christ and enter into His peace, learning to love and serve Him. Several of our Tajik believing friends continue to use their talents to share how Christ has made a positive difference in their lives.

On the first day of March we were driven to the Dushanbe airport, where several friends were waiting to give us last hugs and words of farewell. We knew God was in control, His love stronger than the fiercest winds of change.

On the other end of our journey home, dear Christian friends from the Elmbrook Church in Wisconsin also waited with signs of welcome. From the Milwaukee airport they escorted our family to the home they had lovingly arranged for us. They even furnished us with the use of a mini-van until we could get back on our feet. Even though we had lost a great deal of money by our sudden uprooting, the Father who owns the cattle on a thousand hills continued faithfully to provide.

Our son Justin finished his last two years of high school in the state of Wisconsin. He served on a ministry ship called Logos Hope for two years, then attended Moody Bible Institute in Chicago, Illinois for one year before finishing his college degree at Wheaton College. Justin benefited greatly from growing up in another culture and has continued to relate to people cross-culturally. In the spring of 2017 he traveled to Southeast Asia while pursuing a career in documentary filming around the world.

Rachel, as I mentioned earlier, continues to use her gifts as a teacher and is working on her MA to teach special needs children.

While living and working overseas she learned to relate well to all sorts of people from different cultures—skills which she now uses with the preschoolers she teaches each day. Rachel's supervisors appreciate the quality of care that she shows each child.

Both our son and daughter are now married with families of their own. We have greatly enjoyed the blessings of becoming grandparents. My hope and prayer is that I can be the positive influence that my Aunt Judy and Uncle Lawrence Knutson, former missionaries, were to me.

Around the time that I started to write this book, my beautiful mom, Patricia Carol Olson, who had been diagnosed with lung cancer, started chemo and radiation treatments. She later underwent two operations before passing into Jesus' arms on October 18th, 2015. I had the privilege of being with her on that day in the Lutheran Gunderson Hospital in LaCrosse, Wisconsin. It was a day of intense emotion, but a relief that she was finally with Jesus and other friends and family members who went on ahead of her to heaven.

Although I still miss her very much I am glad she is now free from suffering and all the struggles she had with cigarette and alcohol addictions. Nor does she any longer need to put up with the bickering of people around her. She is in a place of peace with Jesus.

I would like to include the hymn that my Aunt Cheryl and I sang to Mom during the last hours of her life here on earth. As she listened, she praised God with us from her death bed. Soon afterwards she crossed the threshold into eternity.

O the Deep Deep Love of Jesus
(note: this hymn is public domain so should be ok to use)
By S. Trevor Francis

O the deep, deep love of Jesus
Vast, unmeasured, boundless, free
Rolling as a mighty ocean
In its fullness over me
Underneath me, all around me
Is the current of Thy love
Leading onward, leading homeward
To Your glorious rest above

O the deep, deep love of Jesus
Spread his praise from shore to shore
How he loves us, ever loves us
Changes never, nevermore!
How he watches o'er his loved ones,
Died to call them all his own,
How for them he's interceding,
Watching o'er them from the throne!

O, the deep, deep love of Jesus
Love of every love the best!
Tis an ocean vast of blessing,
Tis a haven sweet of rest!
O the deep, deep love of Jesus
Tis heaven of heavens to me,
And it lifts me up to glory,
For it lifts me up to Thee!

A poem that I cherished during those very difficult last days was found clipped to Mom's calendar by the desk in her bedroom. She had been trying to memorize the words. We sang them to the tune of Edelweiss at her funeral.

May the Lord, Mighty God,
Bless and keep you forever,
Grant you peace, perfect peace,
Courage in every endeavor,

Lift up your eyes and see His face
and His grace, forever.
May the Lord, Mighty God,
Bless and keep you forever.

That spring of 2015, Dave and I came to terms with issues in our lives that we needed to embrace without fear. For me that meant fully accepting my past. So I had the privilege of making contact with three more of my half-sisters. Mom's previous boyfriend was their Dad but he abandoned his family because of his alcoholism. I was the oldest among these girls. I have now befriended them, and told them that we share an important life story. I am so grateful that God is a part of that story! He is my best friend and I sincerely hope He will become theirs, too.

CADA—the Central Asian Development Agency--continued on until 2020 when the team sold the "pink" building they operated out of for so many years and the work was finally closed down by the government of Tajikistan. God used this organization to help many thousands of people in that country. But with sadness the team recognized that it was time to move on to other opportunities. Our God was not taken by surprise. He had new and fulfilling plans for us all.

After Word

After we left Tajikistan we kept in contact with a large number of our expatriate and Tajik friends. Dave and I were grateful for communication made possible by Facebook, Instagram, email, Whatsapp, Signal, Telegram, hard copy letters, cell phone and, of course, in- person get-togethers whenever possible, whether over a meal or a cup of coffee.

We also enjoyed making many new friends. Over the next years Dave and I became involved in helping people in Iran with earthquake assistance, as well as developing educational programs and women's empowerment programs for Afghan refugees.

One priority still remains: to know Christ and to make Him known. This has meant equipping and encouraging believers in many different countries to reach out to their neighbors and grow in their trust and faith in Jesus.

As we pursue our ongoing passion to help those who are destitute and living in darkness, we always want to say "yes" to God. As long as He continues to supply the finances, strength and good health we plan to keep being a part of His Great Commission to reach the lost with His love.

On May of 2015, while in Australia on a short speaking tour of churches with my husband Dave, I began to write this book. I was encouraged to see some believers "down under" were reaching out to immigrating Muslims. Tens of thousands have left the suffering they've experienced in their own countries to settle in places where they can live in peace.

Our world today is torn by war and terrorism by groups like Al Qaeda, the Taliban, Al Shabab, the Wahabi movement and ISIS. I am reminded of the book *Simply Jesus* by N.T. Wright, who talks a lot about how Jesus was viewed in the New Testament days and how he is viewed today as an actual historical figure who really did exist. In the Bible the Jesus we see is One who loved people--and He still does, today. He is the only one that can transform people's lives for the better.

In January 2017 Dave and I travelled to Washington DC to attend the National Prayer Breakfast. I felt privileged to be invited to this event, especially in light of the condition our world was in. We were glad to be able to talk with a few members of our government and express some of our opinions about other countries, based on our experience, especially those that are predominately Muslim.

Our thirty-plus years of ministry overseas has been an enormous adventure. All thanks belong to God for His constant mercy and grace. What a privilege to have lived and shared His love in practical ways in India, Pakistan, Bangladesh, Iran and Tajikistan! We are grateful to all the team members that have worked with us over the years. It is important to work together as believers to see the fulfillment of Jesus' Great Commission.

Our prayer is that we stay faithful in serving our Father, wherever we serve others.

We are all born to know Jesus personally and fulfill the plan He has for us. Befriending people we meet along the way is not always easy, but it usually brings a reward beyond our wildest dreams.

As I have continued to become friends with those of other faiths, philosophies, beliefs and persuasions I try to point them to Jesus' way whenever the opportunity arises. If it doesn't arise, I try to just be a friend to them and pray. This means making an effort to spend time with people. I attend their parties, funerals, weddings, circumcision rites, baptisms or other life celebrations. If they invite me to, I pray for people's needs. If they seem interested, I ask if they would like to read God's word together or watch a video about Jesus. Only God can change people's hearts. He also answers prayer and is eager to hear from us. As missionary Elizabeth Elliot once said, "God is interested to help us untie knots, Ask Him for help in all things."

Who are the friends that you hang out with? How can you share God's love with them?

We are all born with the purpose of befriending others.

May this book encourage you to experience the joys of friend-making for yourselves!